FINALS

WILLS

CORE CONCEPTS AND KEY QUESTIONS

Second Edition

T. Leigh Hearn
Series Editor

© 2009 by Kaplan, Inc.

Published by Kaplan Publishing, a division of Kaplan, Inc.
1 Liberty Plaza, 24th floor
New York, NY 10006

Printed in the United States of America

10 9 8 7 6 5 4 3 2 1

ISBN13: 978-1-60714-103-7

Kaplan Publishing books are available at special quantity discounts to use for sales promotions, employee premiums, or educational purposes. Please email our Special Sales Department to order or for more information at kaplanpublishing@kaplan.com, or write to Kaplan Publishing, 1 Liberty Plaza, 24th floor, New York, NY 10006.

I. CAPACITY, INTENT TO MAKE A WILL, AND MISTAKE

A. **DESCRIPTION OF WILL AND CODICIL:** A will is a *written* instrument that is effective only on the testator's death. To be valid, it must be executed (1) by a competent individual, (2) with the requisite testamentary intent, and (3) in accordance with prescribed statutory formalities. This instrument must do one or more of the following:

Dispose of property,

Appoint an executor, or

Revoke (partially or entirely) a prior testamentary document.

A codicil is a written amendment to a will that adds to, alters, revokes, or confirms an earlier will. A codicil must satisfy the same requirements as a will to be valid.

1. **Negative Wills:** Under the traditional common law rule, a testator may not execute a negative will, which is a will that disinherits an heir by words alone. Under this common law rule, to prevent an heir from taking by intestacy, a testator must dispose of all of his assets by devising them to other persons or by transferring them to other persons through will substitutes. However, under § 2-101(b) of the Uniform Probate Code, a testator's will may expressly exclude an individual or a class from intestate succession.

   EXAMPLE: T executes a writing with the requisite testamentary formalities, explicitly disinheriting his only son. If T has not disposed of all of his assets by devising them to other persons or by disposing of them through will substitutes, T's son may take T's estate by intestacy.

   EXAMPLE: T makes a valid will leaving Blackacre to his friend, Clem, and the residue to "his brothers." Subsequently, T executes a codicil to his will that leaves the residue of his estate to his brothers Adam and Carl but expressly excluding Bobby from the residue and from intestate succession. Under the Uniform Probate Code, the codicil will effectively prevent testate distribution to Bobby, because he has been eliminated from the gift of the residue. The codicil will also prevent intestate distribution to Bobby, because T has given the residue of his estate to Adam and Carl and has expressly excluded Bobby from intestate distribution.

2. **Property That May Be Disposed of by Will:** A will may ordinarily dispose of all the property that the testator owns or may alienate.

3. **Persons to Whom a Will May Dispose of Property:** A will may make a disposition of property to virtually any person or legal entity, including: individuals, corporations, unincorporated associations, states, counties, municipalities, the United States or a foreign government. A will may not leave property directly to pets or animals. However, the Uniform Probate Code does permit the establishment of a trust for the care of a designated pet or domestic animal. U.P.C. § 2-907(b).

B. COMPETENCY: In most jurisdictions and under U.P.C. § 2-501, a testator is required to be (1) at least 18 years of age, and (2) of sound mind.

1. **Age Requirement:** In most jurisdictions, a testator must be at least 18 years old. Accord, U.P.C. § 2-501. However, a minor may gain capacity to execute a will through emancipation. A minor may become emancipated through marriage or by court action. If a minor executes a will before she gains capacity to do so, the will may not be admitted into probate unless it is executed with all will formalities after the minor reaches the age of majority or is emancipated.

2. **Sound Mind:** At the time of the performance of any testamentary act, the testator must have sufficient mental capacity. The "sound mind" standard is easier to satisfy than the mental competency required for most other legal acts (e.g., entering into a binding contract). Persons who are mentally disabled or have been adjudged to be incompetent to manage their affairs have been held to be of "sound mind" for purposes of making a will or codicil, provided they otherwise satisfy the standard for testamentary capacity.

   a. **Lack of competence:** A person is not competent to make a will or perform any testamentary act if, at that time, he lacked sufficient mental capacity to be able to (1) understand the nature of the testamentary act, (2) understand and recollect the nature and situation of his property, or (3) remember and understand his relations to his living descendants, spouse, parents, and those whose interests are affected by the will.

      i. **Presumption:** There is a rebuttable presumption that the testator was sane at the time he executed a will that appears valid on its face. The will contestant has the burden of producing evidence that is adequate to overcome this presumption.

      ii. **Admissible evidence:** Evidence pertaining to the testator's conduct before and after the execution of the will is admissible to determine his competency at the time the will was made.

   b. **Insane delusion:** To the extent that a disposition in a person's will is the product of an insane delusion, that devise is invalid. If the overall testamentary scheme is affected by this delusion, the entire will may be invalidated.

      i. **Definition of insane delusion:** A testator executes a will under an insane delusion if the testator persists in believing supposed facts that have no real existence except in his perverted imagination, and he conducts himself accordingly against all evidence and probability.

      ii. **Distinguished from mere mistake:** An insane delusion must be distinguished from a factual error which, though possibly unreasonable, is one which a rational person could have made. A mistake of fact does not constitute a basis for disturbing an otherwise valid will or devise.

iii. **Burden of proof:** The burden of proving an insane delusion is on the party asserting the delusion. A will challenge based on insane delusion is rarely successful.

C. **UNDUE INFLUENCE:** To the extent that the execution or revocation of a will or codicil is the product of undue influence, the will or revocation is ineffective. The test for undue influence is whether such control was exercised over the mind of the testatrix so as to overcome her free agency and free will and to substitute the will of another so as to cause the testatrix to do what she would not otherwise have done but for that control. Requesting, suggesting, advising, or otherwise soliciting (i) a testamentary disposition, or (ii) a change in a prior will made by the testator, does *not* constitute undue influence. The testator's free will must be overcome (and the will must reflect the wishes of the person influencing the testator, rather than the will of the testator).

1. **Pertinent Factors:** In determining whether a will is the product of undue influence, the following factors are considered:

   a. Whether the testator is susceptible to undue influence,

   b. Whether the ultimate disposition of the testator's estate is unnatural, and

   c. Whether the person who allegedly perpetrated the improper conduct had the opportunity to exert undue influence and was motivated or disposed to do so.

2. **Presumption:** The burden of proving undue influence is ordinarily on the will contestant. However, in many states, a presumption of undue influence arises when:

   a. A confidential relationship existed between the testator and the party who exerted the undue influence,

   b. The party who exercised the undue influence played an active role in connection with the execution of the will, *and*

   c. The disposition of the testator's estate is unnatural.

3. **Duress:** A will (or provision thereof) is void to the extent that the testator was induced to act by physical or mental coercion.

4. **Effect of Duress or Undue Influence:** To the extent that the execution or revocation of a will is the product of fraud or undue influence, the will or revocation is void. If only a particular devise is tainted by improper conduct, that particular gift is void. If, however, the duress or undue influence has distorted the testator's overall testamentary scheme, the entire will is a nullity.

D. **FRAUD:** Fraud in the context of probate proceedings consists of the intentional deception of the testator with respect to (i) the nature of the document being signed, (ii) the content of the will, *or* (iii) the facts upon which the will or a particular devise was made.

1. **Fraud in the Inducement:** Fraud in the inducement occurs when a testator is deceived with respect to facts on which he relied in making a (i) will, (ii) disposition, or (iii) partial or complete revocation of an earlier will. The misrepresentation does not have to be perpetrated for the specific purpose of affecting the testator's testamentary scheme. The deceit is sufficient to constitute fraud in the inducement if it was probably relied on by the testator in making, or declining to make, a testamentary gift.

   EXAMPLE: Ann misrepresented to Tim that she was his long lost sister. Tim then executed a will leaving his entire estate to Ann. If Ann intended to induce Tim to execute this will, the will is void. In the absence of intent on Ann's part, the will may also be void if Tim relied on the misrepresentation when he executed the will.

2. **Fraud in the Factum:** Fraud in the factum occurs when the testator is deceived as to the type of the document signed or its contents.

   EXAMPLE: J knows that T has impaired eyesight. J places a will in front of T. T had previously written the document, but had decided not to sign it. J advises T that the document is a letter wishing M (a friend of T's) a "Happy New Year." T's signing of the "letter" would *not* create a valid will, because T lacked the intent to make a testamentary disposition of his property.

   EXAMPLE: J notices that T is preparing a typewritten will. J surreptitiously uses T's typewriter to prepare a new one, making himself the primary devisee. If T fails to notice the change and subsequently executes the document, no will has been made. T lacked the intention to make the writing, as finally constituted and signed, his will.

3. **Effect of Fraud:** When a testamentary fraud has occurred, the court may do whatever is necessary to cure the effects of the improper behavior. The court may:

   a. isolate and invalidate only the affected portions,

   b. invalidate the entire will,

   c. probate the will, but impose a constructive trust upon the affected distribution in favor of the disadvantaged person, or

   d. invalidate a revocation of a will.

   EXAMPLE: T, a Giants' fan, made a will that left his estate to Al and Sara. Sara fraudulently persuaded T that Al was an avid Dodgers fan. Sara knew, however, that Al was a diehard Giants' devotee. As a result, of Sara's deception, T cancelled Al's gift. Because the revocation was procured by fraud, the revocation may be invalidated. Therefore, Al may receive one-half of T's estate.

   EXAMPLE: T intended to leave his estate in equal shares to his two best friends, Jane and Don. However, as a consequence of fraudulent misrepresentations about Jane by Don, T executed a will making Don the sole devisee. Under these circumstances, a court could impose a constructive trust on one-half of Don's share in favor of Jane. It would be unlikely that a court would invalidate the entire will, because invalidation of the entire will would cause T's heirs (rather than Jane and Don) to inherit his estate.

4. **Intestacy or Omission Caused by Fraud:** Fraudulent conduct may cause a person to omit a gift from a will or to refrain from making a will.

   EXAMPLE: T indicates to Alice that she plans to draft a will that leaves her entire estate to Roy, her boyfriend. Because Alice secretly despises Roy, she makes numerous fraudulent misrepresentations about him to T. As a consequence, T refrains from making a will and dies intestate.

   a. **Possible probate court remedies:** There is a division of authority as to the proper remedy in this situation:

      i. One view allows the decedent's estate to pass under intestacy principles. This view is based on a desire to avoid re-writing the decedent's will by ordering the estate to be distributed to the aggrieved person through the imposition of a constructive trust.

      ii. Other courts impose a constructive trust in favor of the aggrieved party when (1) fraud can be proved by clear and convincing evidence, **and** (2) the person who would otherwise receive the intestate's property is the individual who perpetrated the fraud. This result prevents the culpable party from being unjustly enriched.

      iii. Finally, a court may impose a constructive trust when fraud can be proved by "clear and convincing" evidence, even if the persons who would receive the estate under intestacy did **not** participate in the fraud. Arguably, these individuals would be unjustly enriched, even if they benefited only **incidentally** from another's fraud.

   b. **Tort remedies:** When an aggrieved person is **not** made whole by imposition of a constructive trust or similar remedy, that party may sue the culpable individual in tort **for fraud** or **interference with a prospective financial advantage**. As part of the suit, the plaintiff may seek an order enjoining the defendant from receiving any part of the decedent's estate until the litigation is completed. If a plaintiff prevails in a tort action, he may recover any monetary losses and possibly punitive damages, because the defendant acted intentionally.

E. **INTERESTED WITNESSES:** An interested witness is one who has a direct, pecuniary interest in the will. Thus, any witness who receives money or property under a will is "interested."

   1. **Common Law:** At common law, an interested witness was not a competent witness to the will. Therefore, if one of the required witnesses was interested, the will would be denied probate.

2. **Majority Rule:** Under the modern law in most states, the fact that a witness to the will was interested will not void the will, and the will will be admitted to probate. However, by statute in some states, the bequests to the interested witness are purged so that the witness cannot benefit from any influence she or he may have had over the testator. If the interested witness is also an heir under intestate succession, he would take through intestacy even if his gift were purged. In some states, a witness/heir takes the lesser of 1) what he would take under the will or 2) what he would take through intestacy.

   a. **Supernumeraries excluded:** Some states exclude supernumerary witnesses from the purging rule. For example, assume that a will was executed with three witnesses in a jurisdiction that requires two witnesses. The two disinterested witnesses will be used to satisfy the statutory requirement, and the interested witness will be treated as a supernumerary. Therefore, the interested witness will be allowed to take her gift.

   b. **Interested witness presumption:** In some states, if a will is witnessed by a person who is an interested witness, and that person is ***not*** a supernumerary witness, a rebuttable presumption arises that a devise to that witness was obtained by fraud, duress, or undue influence.

3. **Uniform Probate Code:** Under the Uniform Probate Code, the signing of a will by an interested witness does not invalidate the will or any provision of it.

4. The following types of witnesses generally are ***not*** interested witnesses:

   a. **Family members of devisees:** Family members of a devisee are not interested witnesses. Thus, if Pam, Alice's only child and sole beneficiary of Alice's will, witnesses a will under which Alice receives property, Pam is ***not*** an interested witness.

   b. **Persons associated with, or employed by, a devisee:** A person is not an interested witness merely because she is associated with, or even employed by, (i) a person who is a devisee or (ii) a social or business entity that is a devisee. Thus, the president of Elks Lodge #57 is not an interested witness, even though his fraternal association is a major beneficiary under the will that he witnessed.

   c. **Creditors of a devisee:** A creditor of a devisee is not an interested witness.

   d. **Creditors of the decedent:** A creditor of the decedent is not an interested witness. The claims of creditors against a decedent's estate are always paid before any gifts under the will are satisfied.

   e. **Persons designated to perform services for the decedent's estate:** A person is not an interested witness merely because she was appointed by the testator in the will as executor, executrix, accountant, trustee of a trust established in the will, or attorney for the estate. The fees that she might eventually receive must be earned by performing her designated services.

f. **Persons taking a devisee's share under the antilapse provision:** When a person receives a share of the testator's estate because he is a child of a devisee who predeceased the decedent (discussed in detail in the section entitled Distribution of the Testator's Estate), he is ***not*** an interested witness. Under an anti-lapse statute, the recipient does not take under the will but rather takes as a consequence of the application of the antilapse statute.

F. **INTENT NECESSARY TO MAKE A WILL:** For a will or codicil to be valid, the testator must have signed the document with the *present, subjective* intent that it will be operative at his death.

1. **Recitals:** Recitals by the testator (e.g., "I, Mrs. Smith, being of sound mind, hereby execute this document as my last will and testament. . . .") create a **rebuttable presumption** that the writing signed by the testator was intended to be a will. However, this presumption may be rebutted by sufficient evidence showing that the writing was intended for some purpose other than to dispose of the testator's property at her death.

    a. **Sham wills:** A document purporting to be a will lacks the requisite intent when it is made, for example, in jest or only to persuade another of the writer's affection.

    b. **Admissible evidence:** The parol evidence rule does **not** preclude evidence that is inconsistent with a recital that the document is the signator's last will and testament. Extrinsic evidence of the surrounding circumstances and statements made by the purported testator are admissible to show that no testamentary intent was present.

        EXAMPLE: To persuade Jane to marry him, T shows her a holographic will that states that he is leaving his entire estate to her. In fact, T has told numerous people that the purported "will" was simply a ruse to convince Jane of his affection. Because T lacked the intent to make a testamentary devise, the writing is **not** a valid will.

2. **"Present" Testamentary Intent:** The document purporting to be a will must have been intended by the testator to be operational immediately.

    EXAMPLE: T, who currently has no valid will, sends his attorney a handwritten, signed letter. The letter requests T's attorney to prepare a will. The letter also includes a detailed description of how T's estate should be distributed at his death. Pursuant to T's instructions, the attorney drafts a formal will reflecting these dispositions. However, T dies **before** he can come to the attorney's office to sign the document. T has died intestate. Since T specifically requested his attorney to **"prepare a will,"** his letter does not demonstrate a present intent to make a testamentary disposition of his estate.

    EXAMPLE: T sends his niece a handwritten, signed letter, professing his love for her and promising to leave her his entire estate. However, T dies **before** making a will. Because T merely advised his niece of his **intention** to create a will, the requisite **immediate** testamentary intent was lacking.

3. **Conditional Wills:** The effectiveness of a will may be made contingent on the occurrence or nonoccurrence of a prospective event or condition. The will's admission to probate is determined by whether the required event or condition occurred. A will is not effective if it is subject to a condition precedent, such as death from a surgical procedure. However, the will may be given effect if the court considers the conditional language to be merely an expression of the testator's motive for executing the will.

EXAMPLE: The preamble to T's will states that the will is to take effect if T does not survive major surgery that T plans to undergo. If T dies during the surgery, T's will may be admitted to probate. However, if T survives the surgery and later dies from another cause, the will may not be admitted to probate.

a. **Extrinsic proof of conditions:** When a will is unconditional on its face, most courts will **not** permit extrinsic evidence indicating that the testator intended the document to be conditional on the occurrence or nonoccurrence of a subsequent event.

EXAMPLE: T asks his attorney to draw up a will that is unconditional on its face. When T executes the will, he tells his attorney that the will is to take effect if T predeceases his oldest brother. The oral condition may not be proved. Therefore, the will may be admitted to probate, whether T predeceases or survives his oldest brother.

b. **Motive distinguished:** Vague conditional language is likely to be construed as merely an expression of the testator's motive for making the will. If such language is construed as an inducement only, the will may be admitted to probate regardless of whether the condition has been satisfied. If the language is ambiguous, the court may interpret it as inducement to prevent the decedent from dying intestate.

EXAMPLE: T executes a valid will that provides in pertinent part: "I'm going abroad for the summer. If I don't make it back, I want my girlfriend Laura to have everything I own." T puts this will in his wall safe. He returns safely from his trip. However, he dies shortly afterward. The will is still in the safe at T's death. Most courts would prefer to construe the reference to T's trip as merely a statement of T's **motivation** in making the will, especially if T retained the writing subsequent to the inducing event.

4. **Mistake:**

a. **Mistake as to nature of document:** When a person signs a writing that she fails to recognize is a will, the requisite testamentary intent is absent. For example, T may sign a document that she thinks is a letter but that in reality is a will. The will may not be admitted to probate, because T did not have the requisite testamentary intent.

b. **Mistake as to will being signed:** When reciprocal wills are prepared, a testator may mistakenly sign the wrong will. Under the traditional rule, the will is void, because the testator lacked testamentary intent in respect to the document actually executed. However, under the modern approach, the court may reform the document to prevent the testator from dying intestate.

c. **Mistake in the inducement:** Ordinarily, mistakes pertaining to underlying facts on which a testamentary scheme is based may not be remedied. However, some courts recognize an exception to this rule:

   i. **Mistake on face of will:** When (1) the mistake appears on the face of the will, *and* (2) the testator's alternative disposition appears *on the face* of the will, *a court may reform the will* to effectuate the testator's manifested intent. For example, a will may include the following statement: "If John had been alive, I would have left him $1,000." If John was actually alive when the testator executed his will, the court may reform the will to include the gift of $1,000 to John.

d. **Mistake of omission:** Occasionally, a testator inadvertently omits a devise that he intended to make or his attorney neglects to insert a requested provision into the document. Mistake of fact that results in an omission generally does not affect the enforcement of a will. However, some courts may deny probate of a will if the mistake is clear from the face of the will. In addition, the aggrieved devisee may have a negligence action against an attorney who failed to adhere to the testator's instructions.

e. **Mistake as to legal effect of language or law:** When the testator is incorrect as to the legal consequences of his testamentary scheme or the effect of language used in his will, *no* relief is granted. This result is not altered by the fact that the testator relied upon the advice of an attorney in arriving at his erroneous belief.

f. **Textual ambiguities:** The provisions of a will may suffer from a patent or a latent ambiguity.

   i. **Latent ambiguity:** A latent ambiguity exists when the language of a will appears to be unambiguous on its face in describing a beneficiary or property but is actually ambiguous when applied to the facts to which it refers. Extrinsic evidence is admissible to cure a latent ambiguity.

   ii. **Patent ambiguity:** A patent ambiguity exists if the ambiguity is obvious from the face of the will. Traditionally, extrinsic evidence is not admissible to resolve a patent ambiguity. However, under the modern trend, extrinsic evidence may be introduced when a patent ambiguity exists.

EXAMPLE: T leaves Blackacre to "his nephew, George." If T has two nephews whose first names are George, there is a latent ambiguity. Extrinsic evidence is admissible to determine which nephew T most likely had in mind when he made the gift.

EXAMPLE: T's will leaves "one of my diamond rings to Vicky, the other one to Jennifer." Because the will does not differentiate clearly between the two rings, a patent ambiguity exists. Under the modern trend, extrinsic evidence is admissible to resolve this patent ambiguity.

iii. **Falso demonstratio non nocet (an erroneous description does not invalidate):** When a devise contains a description of a person or property that is partially inaccurate, a court may sustain the devise by excising the superfluous, erroneous language.

EXAMPLE: T's will leaves "Blackacre to my niece, Beatrice, who has been a constant source of comfort to me in my declining years, and has cooked me many savory meals." T has two nieces, Betty and Barbara. Betty meets the description in the will. Barbara lived far away from T during the latter years of his life. Under the doctrine of *falso demonstratio non nocet,* a court could strike the word "Beatrice" in T's will. Extrinsic evidence would be available to show that T intended to name Betty as the devisee of Blackacre.

EXAMPLE: T's will leaves "my apartment house in Orange County to Paul." T owns an apartment house, but it is located just over the county line in Los Angeles County. Under the doctrine of *falso demonstratio non nocet,* the words "in Orange County" could be excised. Extrinsic evidence would be admissible to show that T intended Paul to inherit the apartment house.

iv. **Plain meaning rule:** When language in a will is not reasonably susceptible to an assertion of inaccuracy or ambiguity, extrinsic evidence is not admissible to show a different meaning.

EXAMPLE: T's will leaves "Blackacre to my brother Bill." Jill, T's sister who cared for T in his declining years, contends that T actually intended to devise Blackacre to her. Because the meaning of the language used is plain, extrinsic evidence is not admissible to prove that T did intend to leave Blackacre to his sister.

II. WILL FORMALITIES AND COMPOSITION

A. **FORMALITIES REQUIRED FOR A WILL OR CODICIL:** The two main types of testamentary documents are attested (witnessed) and holographic (nonwitnessed) wills. Both of these types of wills generally must be in writing. Oral wills are valid under very limited circumstances.

1. **Statutory Formalities for Attested Wills:** An attested will must satisfy the following formalities:

   a. It must be signed (i) by the testator, or (ii) in the testator's name and presence by another person, who executes the will at the testator's direction,

   b. It must be signed by at least two (or, in a few states, three) competent witnesses who, in the testator's presence and, in some states, in the mutual presence of the other witness[es], witness at least one of the following:

      i. the signing of the will by the testator (or the party signing the document in the testator's name),

      ii. in many states, the testator's acknowledgment of his signature, *or*

      iii. in many states, the testator's acknowledgment of his will, *and*

   c. in some states, each of the signing witnesses understands that he is attesting the testator's will.

   d. Notarized will: In 2008, the Uniform Probate Code was revised to permit the probate of a will that lacks witnesses but that was acknowledged by the testator before a notary public. 2008 revised U.P.C. § 2-502(a)(3)(B). If the will is notarized but is not self-proved, a rebuttable presumption arises that the will satisfies the requirements for execution. 2008 revised U.P.C. § 3-406(2).

   All of the required elements must be present for the requisite formalities to be satisfied.

2. **Analysis of Statutory Elements for an Attested Will:**

   a. **Signature requirement:** The signature requirement is ordinarily viewed in a liberal manner. Partial names, nicknames, and initials have sufficed, provided the court is satisfied that the testator intended to authenticate the document in this manner. Under the Uniform Probate Code, and in most states, the signatures do not have to appear at the end of the document. In some states that require a will to be signed "at the end" the requirement may be satisfied if the signatures are made at the end of the execution process. The exact order of signing among the testator and the subscribing witnesses is not significant, as long as the signatures are made as part of a single, contemporaneous transaction.

   b. **Self-proving affidavit:** A self-proving affidavit is a sworn statement attached to a will that attests that the will was executed in conformity with the applicable state law. The testator and the witnesses sign the affidavit, at the time of execution or at a later date. The signature of the witnesses on the self-proving affidavit may be used to satisfy the requirement of two subscribing witnesses.

A will with a self-proving affidavit may be admitted into probate without further proof.

c. **Attestation requirement:** As noted above, an attested will generally must be witnessed by at least two competent witnesses. Generally, no formal language of attestation is required. Thus, the will may identify the subscribers simply as "witnesses."

  i. **Attestation clause:** However, a formal will often contains an attestation clause. The following language may be used "On the date hereinbelow stated, the undersigned witnessed John Smith sign this document, at which time Mr. Smith advised the undersigned that this was his Last Will and Testament.

  _____ (date)

  _____

  Bob Q. Witness."

  If an attestation clause is signed by the attesting witnesses, a rebuttable presumption arises that the events recited in the clause occurred. 2008 revised U.P.C. § 3-406(3). If the will is witnessed but is not notarized or self-proved, the testimony of at least one of the attesting witnesses is generally required to establish proper execution. However, under the Uniform Probate Code and in some states, if no witness is available, proper execution may be established by other evidence, such as an affidavit of an attesting witness. 2008 revised U.P.C. § 3-406(3).

  ii. **Self-proving affidavit:** A self-proving affidavit is a sworn statement attached to a will that attests that the will was executed in conformity with applicable law. The testator and the witnesses sign the affidavit, at the time of execution or at a later date. Under the Uniform Probate Code, the signature of the witnesses on the self-proving affidavit may be used to satisfy the requirement of two subscribing witnesses. A will with a self-proving affidavit may be admitted into probate without further proof. 2008 revised U.P.C. § 3-406(1). The following language may be used to create a self-proving affidavit that is executed simultaneously with an attested will: I, _____ (name), the testator, sign my name to this instrument this ___ day of _____, ___, and being first duly sworn, do hereby declare to the undersigned authority that I sign and execute this instrument as my will and that I sign it willingly (or willingly direct another to sign for me), that I execute it as my free and voluntary act for the purposes therein expressed, and that I am 18 years of age or older, of sound mind, and under no constraint or undue influence.

d. **Competent witnesses:** A person must be legally competent at the time she witnesses the will. Within this context, "legally competent" means of sufficient maturity and mental capacity to appreciate the significance of witnessing a testamentary disposition. If a witness *subsequently becomes incompetent,* the attestation is still valid. As discussed in the preceding chapter, a witness is not generally disqualified merely because he is "interested."

e. **No formal publication requirement:** In most states, the testator is *not required* to

   (i) make a formal publication of his will by declaring to the witnesses, "This is my will" as he points to the document, or

   (ii) formally request the witnesses to attest the will by saying to each witness, "Now, please witness my will by signing here," as he points to the appropriate place on the document). Attestation may be accomplished in any manner that causes the witnesses to understand that the document they are signing is the testator's will.

f. **"Continuing transaction" requirement:** In most states, the order in which the testator or the attesting witnesses sign a formal will is irrelevant, provided the signings occur in a *contemporaneous* manner. No unreasonable period of time may elapse between fulfillment of the requisite formalities.

   EXAMPLE: T properly signs and publishes his will to Adell and Bart. Adell signs T's will at that time, but Bart fails to sign as a witness until one month later. A court would probably conclude that the "continuing transaction" requirement was not satisfied, and therefore the will was *not* properly executed.

3. **Holographic Wills:** Traditionally, a holographic will has been defined as a will that is entirely in the handwriting of the testator. The Uniform Probate Code expands the definition to include a will with the signature and material portions of the document in the testator's handwriting. U.P.C. § 2-502(b).

Under the U.P.C. and in jurisdictions in which it is recognized, a holographic will is admissible even if it does not bear the signatures of subscribing witnesses.

a. **Testator's signature:** The signature requirement is extremely liberal with respect to a holographic will. The word "Dad," the testator's initials, or simply a first name may constitute a valid signature for a holographic will.

b. **Holographic codicils to attested wills:** If the jurisdiction recognizes holographic wills, a testator may make a holographic codicil to his attested will. Occasionally, a testator attempts to alter his attested will by means of interlineation or marginal notations made on the pages of that document. See the discussion of revocation below for an analysis of whether such an alteration may constitute an effective holographic codicil to an attested will.

c. **Holographic codicils to holographic wills:** Handwritten changes made by the testator to his holographic will *are effective* in most states that recognize holographic wills. The testator is deemed to adopt the prior provisions of his will at the time that the subsequent changes are made.

B. DOCUMENTS COMPROMISING THE WILL

1. **Integration Doctrine:** Writings that are (1) present when the testator executes his will, **and** (2) intended by the testator to be part of the will, may be integrated into the testator's testamentary scheme.

   a. **Presumption:** There is a presumption of integration if (a) pages are **physically connected** in some manner such as by staple or paper clip, or (b) there is a logical continuity in the flow of the will's language from one page to the next.

   b. **Evidence:** Extrinsic evidence is admissible to prove that particular writings, present when the will was made, were intended by the testator to comprise part of the will.

2. **Incorporation by Reference Doctrine:** A writing that *is in existence* when a will or codicil is executed may be incorporated by reference, if the language of the will or codicil (1) manifests this intent, and (2) describes the writing sufficiently to permit its identification.

   EXAMPLE: T executes a will, that states, "I leave the oil paintings in my art collection as indicated in a letter that is to be found in my safe deposit box." The letter may be incorporated by reference into T's will if the letter was in existence when T executed his will. If the letter is incorporated into T's will, the oil paintings will be distributed according to the instructions in the letter. However, if the letter was not in existence when T executed his will, the letter would not be incorporated, and the bequest would fail. In that case, the paintings would pass under the residuary clause of T's will or by intestacy if the will does not include a residuary clause.

   EXAMPLE: T executes a will that bequeaths the books in her library according to a list kept in her strongbox. At that time, the strongbox does contain a list disposing of the books. However, T subsequently destroys that list and places a new one in the strongbox. At that time, the new list cannot be incorporated by reference because it was not in existence when T executed her will. However, if T subsequently executes a codicil to her will, the second letter may be incorporated into the will because the will has been republished by the codicil. (See Revocation and Revival starting on page 16.)

   a. **Application to prior invalid wills:** The incorporation by reference doctrine has been applied *to incorporate a prior invalid will* into a subsequent, properly executed codicil and thereby to give effect to the prior writing.

   Most jurisdictions and the Uniform Testamentary Additions to Trusts Act permit the use of a pour-over provision in a will. Through a pour-over provision, a testator's will "pours over" assets into a trust.

b. **Identity and execution of trust:** A will may pour assets over into a trust if the trust is identified in the testator's will and its terms are set forth in a written instrument other than a will. Some jurisdictions still follow a rule stated in an earlier version of the Uniform Probate Code, which required the trust to be executed before or concurrently with the execution of the testator's will. However, under the current version of the Uniform Testamentary Additions to Trusts Act, as incorporated into the current Uniform Probate Code, the trust may be executed before, concurrently with, or after the execution of the testator's will. U.P.C. § 2-511(a). The trust may also be created in the will of another person, if that person has predeceased the testator.

c. **Funding:** The trust may, but need not, be funded during the life of testator. Assets may be poured over into a funded or unfunded life insurance trust, even if the settlor reserved ownership rights in the insurance contract. U.P.C. § 2-511(a).

d. **Revocability and amendability:** The trust is typically revocable, but it may also be irrevocable. In addition, the trust may be amended after the execution of the testator's will or at the testator's death. However, unless the testator's will provides otherwise, the devise lapses if the trust is revoked or terminated before the testator's death. U.P.C. § 2-511(a).

e. **Property part of trust to which it is devised:** Unless the testator's will provides otherwise, property devised to a trust through a pour-over provision in a will is not held under a testamentary trust of the testator. Instead, the property becomes part of the trust to which it is devised, subject to administration under the provisions of that trust. U.P.C. § 2-511(b).

4. **List of Tangible Personal Property:** The Uniform Probate Code and some states also permit the incorporation of a list disposing of tangible personal property, other than money, that is not otherwise disposed of in the will. To accomplish such an incorporation, the testator must satisfy the following requirements:

   (1) the will must refer to the writing with sufficient specificity;

   (2) the writing must be signed by the testator; and

   (3) the writing must describe the items and the bequests with reasonable certainty. U.P.C. § 2-513.

   The writing does not need to be attached to the will and may be written or changed by the testator throughout his lifetime. The list does not require subscribing witnesses. Multiple lists are permitted. If there is a conflict in dispositions made by multiple lists, the last in time will govern.

5. **"Acts of Independent Significance" Doctrine:** A will may dispose of property by reference to acts and events that have significance apart from their effect on the

dispositions made by the will, whether the acts and events occur before or after the execution of the will, or before or after the testator's death.

EXAMPLE: T's will leaves "$5,000 to each person who is a member of the board of directors of XYZ Corporation" at his death. This document is made six years prior to T's death. When T dies, the five member board of directors of XYZ Corporation is comprised of different persons from those who held office when the will was executed. Under the "acts of independent significance" theory, the new members should each receive $5,000 under T's will, because the appointing and removing directors is a business management act that has a significance apart from its testamentary effect upon T's will.

EXAMPLE: T devises to Elmo "the contents" of her safe deposit box at the time of her death. At the time T executes this will, her safe deposit box contains several personal papers but nothing of marketable value. However, prior to her death, T puts her extensive collection of antique jewelry into the safe deposit box for safe keeping. T placed the jewelry in the box for a purpose that is independent of any testamentary significance. Therefore, Elmo will receive the jewelry.

III. REVOCATION AND REVIVAL

A. **POWER TO REVOKE:** Provided he is competent, a testator *always has the power to revoke his will* and/or any attendant codicils. The fact that the testator has entered into a contract to refrain from revoking his will *does not prevent* him from doing so. The consequences of revoking a will when the testator has contracted to refrain from doing so are described in the section *Contracts Relating to Wills* starting on page 58. As already noted, a revocation procured by fraud, duress, or undue influence is invalid.

B. **METHODS OF REVOKING A WILL:** There are three ways in which a will may be revoked in part or in full.

1. **Revocation by Operation of Law:** Marriage, divorce, and the birth of children each present factual situations under which a person's will may be revoked by operation of law. In many states, a final decree of divorce or annulment automatically revokes the provisions of a will in favor of the former spouse, including powers of appointment and appointments as a fiduciary. For purposes of distribution under the testator's will, the former spouse is viewed as having predeceased the testator.

   a. **Remarriage to former spouse:** If a disposition or other provision in a will in favor of a spouse has been revoked by law as a consequence of divorce or annulment, in most jurisdictions, the gift will be automatically revived by the testator's remarriage to that former spouse.

   b. **Separation:** A will is not revoked if spouses obtain a decree of legal separation that does not terminate the status of husband and wife.

   c. **Life insurance:** Divorce or annulment does ***not*** affect the designation of the former spouse as a beneficiary under a life insurance policy. The insured must cancel the policy or designate a new beneficiary to preclude his former spouse from receiving the proceeds.

      EXAMPLE: T makes a will that devises most of her property to her husband, H, and designates H as the executor of her estate. If T and H divorce prior to her death, the devise to H and his appointment as executor of T's estate are deemed to be revoked in most states.

2. **Revocation by Subsequent Will or Codicil:** A subsequent will or codicil may revoke a prior will (or portion thereof) by

   (i) its express terms, or

   (ii) inconsistency. The document effectuating the revocation must be made with the requisite formalities of a valid will or codicil, but it need not be the same type of instrument as the document it revokes or modifies. For example, a valid holographic revocation may revoke a prior attested will. A subsequent testamentary document that does not expressly revoke a prior one is treated as a codicil to the first and revokes the first will only to the extent that it varies or contradicts the terms of the first will.

      EXAMPLE: T executes a valid will. He later executes a typed document containing a clause that expressly revokes the first will. This typed document is witnessed by only one competent person. However, in this jurisdiction, two competent witnesses are required. Because it was not executed properly, the second document does not revoke T's validly executed will.

      EXAMPLE: T executes a valid will devising her car to Jim and Blackacre to Bill. T subsequently executes a valid will that leaves "all of my property" to Mike. The second will does not contain an express revocation of the gifts to Jim and Bill. However, the second will is inconsistent with the first, because it gives T's entire estate to Mike. Therefore, the first will is revoked by inconsistency. Because any earlier devises are "inconsistent" with a gift of "all" of T's property, the initial will may be revoked by inconsistency.

      EXAMPLE: T's will leaves Blackacre to Paul and the residue of T's estate to Annette. Subsequently, T makes a codicil that leaves $5,000 to Harvey. Although the devise to Harvey would decrease the amount of the residue passing to Annette, the codicil is not inconsistent with the overall disposition of T's estate. Therefore, the codicil does not revoke the will.

3. **Revocation by Physical Act:** A will, or a portion thereof, may be revoked by burning, tearing, cancellation, obliteration, or other means of destruction; ***provided***

   (i) the act is performed on the will (or an executed duplicate), and

(ii) the act is accompanied by the testator's present intent to revoke the will (or portion thereof). In many states, the physical act may be done by another person, if the act is accomplished in the testator's presence and at his direction. The Uniform Probate Code also permits the act to be done in the testator's conscious presence, which does not need to be in the testator's line of sight. U.P.C. § 2-507(a)(2) and comment.

a. **Description of physical acts constituting revocation:** Under this traditional rule, the act must touch material words of the will. However, the act is not required to obliterate completely the affected words. In contrast, if intent to revoke is clear, the Uniform Probate Code permits revocation by an act that does not touch a material portion of the will. U.P.C. § 2-507(a)(2).

b. **A revocation by physical acts upon testator's signature:** When the testator burns, cancels, tears off, or obliterates his signature, with the necessary intent, the will is revoked in its entirety.

c. **Partial revocation by physical act:** Some jurisdictions do not permit partial revocation by physical act, such as crossing out one clause in a will. However, other jurisdictions follow the Uniform Probate Code in permitting partial revocation by act. U.P.C. § 2-507(a)(2).

d. **Necessary intent:** Concurrently with his physical act, the testator must have the intention to revoke. If the testator mistakenly or accidentally does any of the physical acts described above to his will, no revocation occurs. When the testator revokes a will by physical act with the necessary intent, but then changes his mind, he must comply with the necessary testamentary formalities to reinstate the will.

e. **Presumptions and inferences pertaining to lost or mutilated wills:**

   i. **Lost wills:** If the testator's will was last seen in the testator's possession, the testator was competent until death, and neither the will nor a duplicate original of the will can be found after the testator's death, it is presumed that the testator destroyed the will with the intent to revoke it.

   ii. **Mutilated wills:** If the will was last seen in the testator's possession or control, and it is found after the testator's death in a mutilated condition, there is an inference that the testator mutilated it with the requisite intent to revoke.

   iii. **Inadvertently lost or destroyed wills:** When there is evidence that the testator's will was *inadvertently lost or destroyed,* no revocation has occurred. Evidence of the will's provisions is admissible to probate, but there must be sufficient proof of its (i) valid execution, and (ii) contents.

   EXAMPLE: T executes a valid will. He subsequently decides he wants to change the part of his will disposing of his stamp collection. T cuts off the last paragraph on page "3" of his will, which contained the devise of his stamp collection to his nephew, N. T types up a new paragraph, devising the stamp collection to his brother, B. T then tapes this new provision to page "3" of his will, at the place where the former provision had been removed. The portion of page "3" that was cut off has been revoked. Assuming the necessary formalities have **not** been undertaken with respect to the new paragraph added to page "3," the devise to B is **not** valid.

EXAMPLE: T rips up an *unexecuted copy* of his will. He informs numerous people who watch him perform this act that he is canceling his present will and desires to die intestate. No revocation has occurred. Although T intended to revoke his will, the act was performed on an *unexecuted* duplicate.

EXAMPLE: T's will bequeaths to Gloria $5,000 and T's 14-karat gold watch. Subsequently, T becomes disenchanted with Gloria and lines out the words pertaining to the timepiece. The revocation is effective. The gold watch will pass under the residuary clause in T's will (or by intestacy if there is no residuary clause).

EXAMPLE: T's will leaves Cynthia $10,000. T becomes disenchanted with Cynthia and lines out the final zero (0), seeking to reduce her bequest to $1,000. T's reduction of Cynthia's gift is valid. The additional $9,000 will pass under the residuary clause (or by intestacy if there is no residuary clause).

f. **Effect of partial revocation on other gifts:** Partial revocation by physical act cannot be used to *increase* a gift or to *re-allocate it to another devisee* (except indirectly by allowing the revoked gift to fall into the residue). To increase a specific or general devise, or to allocate it to others, a testator must comply with the requisite testamentary formalities. When a gift has been made to multiple specific or general devisees, revoking the devise to one of the recipients does not (absent the requisite testamentary formalities) result in an enhancement of the gifts to the other devisees.

EXAMPLE: T's will leaves Blackacre to Bob and Warren, as tenants in common. The residuary clause passes the residue of T's estate to Warren. Subsequently, T becomes disenchanted with Warren and lines out the latter's name with the intention of revoking the gift to Warren and leaving Blackacre entirely to Bob. While Warren's gift is canceled, the gift to Bob is not increased. To increase Bob's gift, T would have to comply with the applicable testamentary formalities. Thus, Bob and Warren would each own an undivided one-half interest in Blackacre.

EXAMPLE: T devised: "Blackacre to M for life, the remainder to C." T later decided to devise to M a fee simple interest in Blackacre. T lined out all of the words in the clause after, "Blackacre to M.... " An increase in a devise may not be accomplished through partial revocation by physical act. Therefore, on T's death, M will take only a life estate in Blackacre. T did intend to revoke the remainder gift to C. Therefore, on T's death, the remainder interest will pass via the residuary clause of T's will or under intestacy principles.

4. **Codicil/Will Interface**

   a. **Revocation of codicil:** The revocation of a codicil *does not revoke the will,* even if there is extrinsic evidence that the testator intended a revocation.

   EXAMPLE: T made a valid will that left his entire estate to Martha. Shortly thereafter, T made a codicil that left Blackacre to Carl. Subsequently T tore up the codicil, announcing that he intended to die intestate. The will in favor of Martha is still effective.

   b. **Revocation of will:** The revocation of a will revokes all codicils to that will. However, when the codicil is sufficiently complete to constitute a will and the testator *intends* the codicil to be treated separately, the codicil remains effective.

   EXAMPLE: T makes a valid will that leaves his entire estate to Ralph. Sometime later, T makes a codicil that leaves Blackacre to Alice. Blackacre is the only asset of significance in T's estate. T subsequently writes "Canceled" across the first page of his will. After T dies, the burden of proof will be on Alice to show that T intended the codicil to remain in effect. If Alice cannot prove this intent, T's estate, including Blackacre, will pass under intestacy principles.

5. **Revival**

   a. **Re-execution or re-acknowledgment:** When an earlier, revoked will is re-executed or re-acknowledged with the necessary testamentary formalities, the earlier will is revived. The earlier will *must* still be in existence for this doctrine to apply.

   EXAMPLE: T revokes his will by writing a large "X" on the face of each page with the intent to cancel the document. He later decides to reinstate this will. He re-executes the document before two competent witnesses, who, understanding that the writing is T's will, sign it. The document is once again effective as T's will, as of the date it was re-executed.

   b. **Republication by codicil:** An earlier, valid will may be republished by a reference to it in a subsequent codicil. The date of the codicil becomes the effective date of the republished will. Republication may be accomplished even if the earlier will was revoked.

      i. **Prior revoked will must be extant:** To be republished by reference, a prior revoked will must still be in existence at the time of the republication.

      ii. **Republication language is not necessary:** The republishing codicil need not include specific language of republication. Rather, the codicil need only reference the prior will. For example, republication may be accomplished with the following language: "This document is a codicil to my will dated 1 January 2000."

iii. **Prior will must have been validly executed:** To be republished by reference, a will must have been validly executed. However, an earlier, invalid document may be given effect under the "incorporation by reference" doctrine.

EXAMPLE: T makes a will on January 1, 1999. He subsequently revokes it by drawing lines through each of the provisions. Nevertheless, the original words are legible. Afterwards, T executes a valid codicil, which states, "This is a codicil to my will of January 1, 1999." The previously revoked will is deemed to be republished as of the date of the codicil.

c. **Doctrine of dependent relative revocation:** Dependent relative revocation may be found if the testator revokes a will based on the mistaken belief that a subsequently executed will is valid. Dependent relative revocation is based on the presumption that a decedent would prefer to die testate rather than intestate. To determine that preference, the court may consider evidence of the testator's schemes of distribution. Intent to die testate may be found if the several wills contain similar schemes of distribution. In contrast, intent to die testate may not be found if the several wills contain markedly different schemes of distribution.

i. **Doctrine rarely applied to an attempt to diminish a gift:** DRR may be used to restore a devise that had been revoked when the testator attempted to substitute a larger gift for the devisee. However, DRR is rarely used when the testator revoked a devise and attempted to substitute a smaller gift for the devisee. Because the testator sought to diminish the gift, the court infers that he would prefer the devisee to take nothing (rather than the original gift).

ii. **Revoked will need not be extant:** Dependent relative revocation may be applied even if the original will is no longer in existence. However, execution and terms of the revoked will must be proven.

EXAMPLE: T makes a valid will disposing of his estate. Subsequently, he makes another attested will identical in content to his first will, except that he changes the executor from Paul to John. At the time the second document is executed, T writes "Canceled" across the initial page of the first will with the intent to revoke it. The second will, however, is ineffective because it was witnessed by only one person. The first will was revoked simultaneously with the attempted new one. In addition, T would probably have preferred probate of the first to intestacy, because the second will changed only the executor. Therefore, DRR may be applied, and the first will may be admitted to probate.

EXAMPLE: T, a widower, devises his entire estate to his girlfriend, Diana. Subsequently, T burns that will and immediately signs a new will leaving everything to his three children. However, the second will is not made with the requisite testamentary formalities. The distribution schemes in the two wills are markedly different. Therefore, DRR will not be applied, and T's estate will pass by intestacy.

EXAMPLE: Under T's valid will, John receives a devise of $10,000. Wishing to increase the gift to John, T draws a line through the $10,000 figure and writes "$15,000" over it. The attempted gift to John of $15,000 *is not effective,* because it was not accompanied by the requisite formalities. However, a partial revocation by act has been accomplished by the line drawn through the $10,000 sum contained in the will. DRR will be applied to preserve the gift to John, because the testator sought to increase the gift to John. Therefore, John will take $10,000.

EXAMPLE: T executes a valid will that leaves $10,000 to Art. Subsequently, T attempts to reduce Art's gift to $1,000 by drawing a line through the "$10,000" figure and writing $1,000 above it. The attempt to devise $1,000 to Art is ineffective, because it is not accompanied by the requisite formalities. However, a partial revocation by act has been accomplished by the line drawn through the $10,000 sum contained in the will. DRR will not be applied in this case, because the testator sought to diminish the gift to Art. Therefore, the gift to Art will be revoked, and Art will take nothing.

EXAMPLE: T executed a valid will that left everything to Joy. Subsequently, T wrote "Canceled" across the first page of his will with the intent to revoke it. Simultaneously, T made a new valid will, leaving everything to Alice. T then died, with the second will in effect. Because the second will is valid, DRR does not apply. Therefore, Alice will take T's estate.

IV. ESTATES AND FUTURE INTERESTS

An estate in land is an interest in real property that is presently or may become possessory.

A. PRESENT POSSESSORY ESTATES:

1. **Fee Simple Absolute:** O conveys "to A and his heirs." A fee simple absolute is the largest possible estate in land. The fee simple absolute represents the aggregate of all possible rights that a person may have in that parcel of land, including (1) the right to sell or convey all or part of the property; and (2) the right to devise the property. A fee simple absolute may last in perpetuity. If the owner of a fee simple absolute dies intestate, the property will pass to the owner's heirs by intestate succession. The following words are used traditionally to create a fee simple absolute: O conveys "to A and his heirs." At early common law, the words "to A and

his heirs" were required to create a fee simple absolute. However, under modern law, a fee simple absolute is generally presumed when the words "to A" are used.

2. **Fee Tail:** O conveys "to A and the heirs of his body." At early common law, a fee tail was a freehold estate that descended to the grantee's lineal descendants only. The fee tail was followed by a reversion in the grantor or a remainder in a third party. (See the discussion of future interests below.) The future interest fell in if and when the grantee's lineal line failed. Today, if the words "to A and the heirs of his body" are used, in most jurisdictions, the grantee receives a fee simple absolute. However, in some states, the grantee has a life estate, with a remainder per stirpes in the grantee's lineal descendants in being at the time of the life tenant's death.

3. **Life Estate:** O conveys "to A for life." A life estate lasts for the duration of the grantee's life. A life estate per autre vie is an estate in one person that is measured by the life of another person.

   EXAMPLE: O conveys "to A for the life of B." If B predeceases A, A's estate ends at B's death. If A predeceases B, under the modern rule, A's heirs take until B dies.

   a. **Waste:** The possessor of a life estate (or a leasehold interest) has the right to possess, use, and enjoy the property during the duration of her estate. However, she may not do anything that affects adversely the future interest that follows the life estate. An act that affects the future interest adversely is called waste.

      i. **Voluntary or affirmative waste:** Voluntary waste consists of the voluntary commission of an act that causes more than a trivial injurious effect on or change in the property. The following exceptions are recognized to the voluntary waste rules: natural resources may be consumed (1) for the repair and maintenance of the property, (2) with permission, or (3) under the open mines doctrine. The open mines doctrine is based on prior exploitation and applies to both life tenants and tenants for years.

      ii. **Permissive or involuntary waste:** Involuntary waste occurs if the life tenant or leasehold tenant permits the premises to fall into disrepair. Involuntary waste may also occur if the life tenant fails to pay mortgage interest payments, taxes, or the tenant's share of special assessments.

         (a) **Life tenant's duty to repair:** A life tenant has a duty to maintain the property in a reasonable state of repair, ordinary wear and tear excepted. The life tenant's duty in respect to permissive waste is only to the extent of the income derived, or, if she personally occupies the premises, to the extent of the reasonable rental value of the land.

         (b) **Mortgages:** The life tenant has a duty to pay the interest on a mortgage, to the extent of profits derived from the property.

(c) **Taxes:** The life tenant must pay all ordinary taxes, to the extent of profits derived from the property.

(d) **Special assessments:** The life tenant must pay the full cost (apparently to the extent of income derived) if the life of the public improvement is less than the duration of the life tenant's estate. Equitable apportionment is applied for improvements likely to last longer (e.g., curbs and streets).

iii. **Ameliorative (or meliorative, ameliorating, or meliorating) waste:** Ameliorative waste occurs if an act of a life tenant increases the value of the premises. Traditionally, ameliorative waste was prohibited. However, under modern law, a life tenant may now commit ameliorative waste if (1) it is permissive, (2) the market value of the remainderman's interest is not impaired, or (3) a substantial and permanent change in the neighborhood has deprived the property of a reasonable current value.

iv. **Standing to sue for waste:** A holder of a reversion has standing to sue for past or future waste. A vested remainderman also has standing to sue for past or future waste. However, a contingent remainderman has standing to sue to prevent future waste but not for damages for past waste. Authorities question whether the holder of a possibility of reverter or right of reentry or executory interest has standing to sue for waste.

4. **Defeasible Estates:** A defeasible estate is an estate that may terminate before its maximum duration has run.

a. **Determinable estates:** A determinable estate terminates automatically on the happening of a named future event. A determinable estate is described with the following words: for so long as, during, while, until. A determinable estate is created (1) in one clause, and (2) with a limitation built into that one clause.

Example of fee simple determinable: O conveys "to A and his heirs for so long as the premises are used as a farm."

Example of life estate determinable: O conveys "to A for life while the premises are used for recreational purposes."

i. **Accompanying future interest:** A determinable estate is followed by a possibility of reverter, which may be implied. (See the discussion below.)

b. **Estates subject to a condition subsequent:** An estate subject to a condition subsequent may be cut short if the estate is retaken by the grantor or a third person on the happening of a named future event. An estate subject to a condition subsequent is described with the following words: provided however, however if, on condition that, in the event that. An estate subject to a condition subsequent is created (1) in two separate clauses, and (2) with a condition stated in the second clause.

Example of fee simple subject to condition subsequent: O conveys "to A and his heirs, but if the premises are used for commercial purposes, then O has the right to reenter the premises and terminate A's estate."

Example of life estate subject to a condition subsequent: O conveys to A for life; provided, however, that if the premises are not used for charitable purposes, O may reenter and retake the premises.

c. **Fee simple subject to executory interest:** A fee simple subject to an executory interest is an estate that is defeased in favor of a third person on the happening of a named event.

EXAMPLE: O conveys "to A for so long as the premises are used for agricultural purposes, but if the premises cease to be used for agricultural purposes, then to B."

EXAMPLE: O conveys "to A, but if liquor is served on the premises, then to B."

i. **Accompanying future interest:** A fee simple subject to an executory interest is followed by a shifting executory interest.

d. **Rules of construction and preferences:** If the words of the grant are not clear, a covenant is preferred over a defeasible estate, because the award is money damages rather than forfeiture. Further, a fee simple subject to a condition subsequent is preferred over a fee simple determinable, because forfeiture is not automatic in the former estate.

B. FUTURE INTERESTS

1. **Reversionary Interests:** Reversionary interests remain in the grantor or the testator's estate.

a. **Reversions:** A reversion is a future interest retained by the grantor when the grantor transfers less than a fee interest to a third person. Under the majority rule, a reversion is transferable, devisable, and descendible. A reversion is not subject to the Rule Against Perpetuities (RAP).

EXAMPLE: O conveys "to A for life, then to B for life, then to C for life." The entire fee simple absolute is not accounted for in this transaction. Therefore, following all of these life estates, O has a reversion.

EXAMPLE: O conveys "to A for life." O retains a reversion. If O then conveys her reversion to C, C's interest is still defined as a reversion, even though it is now in a third party.

EXAMPLE: T devises Blackacre "to A for life," and T also devises "the rest and residue of my estate to B." When T dies, (1) A gets a present possessory life estate, and (2) B gets the residue of T's estate, which includes the reversion to Blackacre.

b. **Possibilities of reverter:** A possibility of reverter is a future interest in the grantor that follows a determinable estate. At strict common law, a possibility of reverter could descend through intestacy but could not be devised or transferred inter vivos. Under the modern trend, a possibility of reverter is transferable, devisable, and descendible. The statute of limitations begins to run on a possibility of reverter as soon as the limitation occurs, because the property automatically reverts to the grantor on the occurrence of the limitation. A possibility of reverter is not subject to RAP.

EXAMPLE: O conveys "to A and her heirs for so long as gambling does not occur on the premises." A has a fee simple determinable. O has a possibility of reverter, which is implied, and which falls in automatically if gambling occurs. If O then conveys her possibility of reverter to C: C's interest is still defined as a possibility of reverter, even though it is now in a third party.

c. **Rights of reentry (powers of termination):** A right of reentry is a future interest in the grantor that follows an estate subject to a condition subsequent. At strict common law, a right of reentry could descend through intestacy but could not be devised or transferred inter vivos. Today, a right of reentry is descendible. Under the modern majority rule, a right of reentry is devisable but is not transferable inter vivos. Under the modern minority rule, a right of reentry is transferable, devisable, and descendible. The statute of limitations does not begin to run against a right of reentry until the grantor attempts to exercise the right. However, in some states, the statute of limitations begins to run against a right of reentry when the condition occurs. A right of reentry is not subject to RAP.

EXAMPLE: O conveys "to A and his heirs, but if boxing matches are held on the premises, then O and his heirs may reenter and terminate A's estate." A has a fee simple on an executory limitation, and O has a right of reentry. If boxing matches are presented on the premises, O must take affirmative steps before A's estate is terminated. If O fails to reserve expressly a right of reentry, if and when boxing matches are presented, O may be powerless to reclaim the property. If O then transfers her right of reentry to C (in a jurisdiction that permits inter vivos transfers of rights of reentry): C's interest is still defined as a right of reentry, even though it is now in a third party.

EXAMPLE: O conveys "to A; provided, however, that liquor may not be served on the premises." No right of re-entry has been reserved. Therefore, O cannot take the property back if liquor is served on the premises. The condition subsequent language will be stricken. Therefore, A is left with a fee simple absolute.

2. **Remainders**

a. **Vested remainders:** A remainder is a future interest created in and that remains away from the grantor in a third person. A vested remainder requires its takers to be ascertained or ascertainable at the time that the remainder is created. A vested remainder also must fall in automatically at the natural termination of the previous estate, which means that there are no conditions precedent to taking. A vested remainder is transferable, descendible, and devisable. A fully vested remainder is not subject to RAP. However, a remainder that is vested subject to open is subject to RAP.

CHARACTERISTICS OF FUTURE INTERESTS IN THE GRANTOR			
	Reversion	**Possibility of Reverter**	**Right of Reentry**
Corollary Present Estate	Life estate, fee tail	Determinable estate	Estate subject to condition subsequent
Alienable	Yes	Yes	No (majority rule)
Devisable	Yes	Yes	Yes
Descendible	Yes	Yes	Yes
Subject to RAP	No	No	No

EXAMPLE: Testator devises "to A for life, remainder to B and his heirs." A has a life estate. B has a vested remainder in fee simple, because (1) the taker is identified, and (2) B's interest falls in automatically at the natural termination of the previous estate (when A dies).

EXAMPLE: O conveys "to A for life, remainder to B for life, remainder to C and her heirs." A has a life estate, B has a vested remainder for life and C has a vested remainder in fee simple.

i. **Vested remainder subject to open** (sometimes called vested subject to partial divestment): A remainder that is vested subject to open is a remainder that (1) has been made to a class (e.g., "my children") and (2) has at least one member who is ascertainable and who has satisfied any conditions precedent to vesting.

EXAMPLE: T devises "to A for life, remainder to B's children and their heirs." If, at the time of creation (which is T's death), B is living and has one child, C, (1) A has a present possessory life estate, (2) C has a vested remainder subject to open, because B could have more children, and (3) T retains nothing. If, one year later, a second child, D, is born to B (1) A has a life estate, (2) C and D together have a vested remainder subject to open, and (3) T retains nothing.

ii. **Vested remainder subject to total divestment:** A vested remainder subject to total divestment is presently vested but may be terminated on the happening of a future event.

> **EXAMPLE:** O conveys "to A for life, remainder to B for so long as the premises are used as a camp for underprivileged children." A has a life estate, B has a vested remainder subject to total divestment, and O retains a possibility of reverter.

b. **Contingent remainders:** A remainder is a future interest that is created in and that remains away from the grantor in a third person. A remainder will be contingent if (1) the takers are unascertained, or (2) the interest is subject to a condition precedent and does not fall in automatically on the natural termination of the previous estate. At strict common law, a contingent remainder could descend and be devised but could not be transferred inter vivos. Under modern law, a contingent remainder is transferable, descendible, and devisable (except, possibly, when the contingent remainder is in an unascertained person). A contingent remainder is subject to RAP.

> **EXAMPLE:** T devises "to A for life, remainder to A's first-born daughter and her heirs." If, at the time of creation, A is living, A has a life estate. If A does not yet have a daughter, A's first-born daughter has a contingent remainder in fee simple, because the taker is not yet ascertained or ascertainable. Therefore, T's estate retains a reversion.

> **EXAMPLE:** O conveys "to A for life, remainder to B and her heirs if B graduates from law school." If, at the time of creation, B has already graduated from law school, A has a life estate and B has a vested remainder in fee simple. If, at the time of creation, B has not yet graduated from law school, A has a life estate and B's remainder is contingent, because B has not yet fulfilled the condition precedent of graduating from law school. Therefore, O retains a reversion.

c. **Destructibility of contingent remainders:** Under traditional common law, a legal contingent remainder in real property is destroyed in the following situations.

i. **Failure to vest:** A contingent remainder is destroyed if it fails to vest by the natural termination of the prior vested estate.

> **EXAMPLE:** O conveys "to A for life, remainder to B and her heirs if B opens a veterinary clinic." A has a life estate. If B has not yet opened a veterinary clinic, B has a contingent remainder, which is contingent on B opening the clinic, and O retains a reversion. If A dies and B has not yet opened a veterinary clinic, (1) B's contingent remainder cannot fall in naturally at the termination of A's life estate, because B has not yet met the condition precedent to vesting (opening the clinic); (2) B's contingent remainder is destroyed; and, (3) therefore, O's reversion will fall in.

ii. **Merger:** A contingent remainder is also destroyed when one party who possesses a present or future interest in the subject realty by subsequent transactions obtains all outstanding present and vested estates in that property: (1) by surrender of the present estate to the owner of a future estate; (2) by release of a future estate to the owner of a present estate; or (3) when all holders of present and future vested interests convey all of these interests to a third party.

EXAMPLE: O conveys "to A for life, remainder to B if B earns a doctorate in psychology." A has a life estate. If B has not yet earned a doctorate in psychology, B has a contingent remainder in fee simple absolute, and O retains a reversion. If, one year later, O conveys her reversion to A and B still has not earned a doctorate in psychology, A now has both a life estate and a reversion. At common law, A's two interests merge, because they are not separated by a vested estate. Thus, A gets a fee simple absolute, and B's contingent remainder is destroyed.

EXAMPLE: O conveys "to A for life, remainder to B's grandchildren." A has a life estate. If B does not yet have a grandchild, B's unborn grandchild has a contingent remainder, and O retains a reversion. If O later devises his reversion to A and B still does not have a grandchild at the time of O's death, (1) at O's death, A receives O's reversion, and (2) A also has her life estate. A's two interests merge, because they are not separated by a vested estate. Therefore, A gets a fee simple absolute, and the contingent remainder in B's grandchildren is destroyed.

EXAMPLE: T devises "to A for life, remainder to A's widow." T's will creates this devise but does not expressly dispose of the reversion. However T's will leaves the residue of T's estate to A. At the time the will takes effect, A is alive and married. At T's death, (1) A has a life estate and a reversion; (2) A's widow has a contingent remainder (because a person cannot have a widow or widower until he or she dies); and (3) the contingent remainder of A's widow is not destroyed by merger, because A's interests were created at the same time and by the same instrument. If, one year after T dies, A conveys his life estate and the reversion to C, C gets a life estate and a reversion. The life estate and the reversion merge, giving C a fee simple absolute and destroying the contingent remainder in A's widow.

iii. **Forfeiture:** If the holder of the present possessory estate forfeits her interest before the contingent remainder vests.

iv. **Abolition of destructibility:** Under modern law, many jurisdictions have abolished the rule of destructibility of contingent remainders. In those jurisdictions, if a contingent remainder has not vested at the natural termination of the prior vested estate, the contingent remainder will become an executory interest. (See the discussion below.)

3. **Executory Interests:** An executory interest is a future interest in a third person that cannot fall in automatically at the natural termination of the previous estate, because (1) it cuts off the previous estate (shifting executory interest), or (2) it does not become presently possessory until some time after the natural termination of the previous estate (springing executory interest). An executory interest is transferable, descendible, and devisable. An executory interest is subject to RAP.

EXAMPLE: O conveys "to A, but if skateboarding occurs on the premises then to B and her heirs." A has a fee simple subject to an executory limitation. B has a shifting executory interest, because his interest may cut short A's estate.

CHARACTERISTICS OF REMAINDERS			
	Fully vested	**Vested subject to open**	**Contingent**
Alienable	Yes	Yes	Yes
Devisable	Yes	Yes	Yes
Descendible	Yes	Yes	Yes
Standing to sue for waste	Yes	Yes	No
Right to compel holder of present estate to pay taxes and interest	Yes	Yes	No
Subject to RAP	No	Yes	Yes

EXAMPLE: O conveys "to A for life, remainder to A's children and their heirs one week after A's death." A has a life estate. A's children have a springing executory interest, because their interest cannot become presently possessory until one week after the natural termination of A's life estate. O retains a reversion. After A's death, O's reversion falls in and then, one week after A's death, the fee simple springs out of O to A's children.

4. **Distinguishing Contingent Remainders from Executory Interests:** In jurisdictions that have retained the destructibility rule, contingent remainders, which are destructible, must be distinguished from executory interests, which are not destructible. If it is possible that a future interest may fall in at the natural termination of the previous estate, the interest will be treated for all purposes as a contingent remainder.

EXAMPLE: O conveys "to A for life, remainder to B and his heirs if B reaches 30." A has a life estate. If B is not yet 30 at the time of creation, B may not be ready to take when A dies. However, B could possibly turn 30 before A dies. Therefore, B's interest is treated as a contingent remainder rather than an executory interest. Thus, B's interest may be destroyed in states in which contingent remainders are still destructible.

EXAMPLE: O conveys "to A for so long as the premises are used for conservation purposes, but if the premises are not used for conservation purposes, then to B and her heirs." A has a fee simple on an executory limitation. B will take only if A's estate is cut short by the failure to use the premises for conservation purposes. Thus, B cannot possibly take at the natural termination of A's estate. Therefore, B has shifting executory interest rather than a contingent remainder.

C. CONSTRUCTIONAL RULES

1. **Rule in Shelley's Case:** O conveys "to A for life, remainder to the heirs of A."

   The Rule in Shelley's Case applies if the following elements are present: (1) A must receive a freehold estate (a life estate or a fee tail); (2) A's heirs must receive a remainder in fee (or in tail); (3) the same instrument must create both A's and A's heirs' interests; and (4) both estates must be legal or both must be equitable. If all of these requirements are met, (1) A receives both a life estate and a remainder, and (2) by merger A receives a fee simple. Thus, A's heirs' take nothing on their own. The Rule in Shelley's Case is a rule of law, which the court must treat as creating an irrebuttable presumption. The Rule in Shelley's Case has been abolished by statute or judicial decision in most states.

2. **Doctrine of Worthier Title:** O conveys "to A for life, remainder to the heirs of O."

   The Doctrine of Worthier Title may apply if the following elements are present: (1) A must receive an estate less than a fee simple, such as a life estate or a term of years; (2) O's heirs must receive a remainder (or an executory interest, in the rare case); (3) both interests must be created by the same instrument; and (4) both interests must be legal or both must be equitable. The Doctrine of Worthier Title has been abolished in many states. In states that continue to recognize it, the doctrine applies to inter vivos transfers only. The creation of a remainder O's heirs raises a rebuttable presumption that O intended to retain that interest as a reversion. This presumption may be rebutted by clear express evidence that O did intend to create a remainder in his heirs. If the presumption is raised, but it is not rebutted, A receives a life estate and O retains a reversion. Thus, O's heirs take nothing on their own.

3. **Rule of Convenience:** Under the Rule of Convenience, a class closes when a member of the class is entitled to distribution. The Rule of Convenience applies to the following classes: "children," "grandchildren," "brothers," "sisters," "nephews," "nieces," "cousins," "issue," "descendants," or "family" of a designated person.

   a. **Immediate gift to a class (with no condition precedent):** If the class is already closed at the time the gift takes effect (which is the time of conveyance for an inter vivos gift or time of testator's death for a will), all members of the class will take. If, at the time the gift takes effect, the class has members entitled to take immediately but the class has not previously closed, all members of the class conceived at the time the gift is made will be included in the class and may take. However, the class will close to the exclusion of after-born children, who may not take. If the class has no members at the time the gift is made, all members of the class, whenever born, will be included and may take.

EXAMPLE: T devises "to the sons of A."

i. If A is dead at the time of T's death, the class of A's sons will be closed. Therefore, all of A's sons will be included and may take.

ii. If A is alive at the time of T's death and has sons at that time, the sons born at the time of T's death are entitled to immediate distribution. Therefore, the class will close, and all of those sons will be included and may take. However, after-born sons will be excluded.

iii. If A is alive at T's death but does not have sons at that time, no one is then entitled to immediate distribution. Therefore, the class should remain open. All of A's sons, whenever born, will be included and should be able to take. Some authorities suggest that the first-born son takes the entire estate on his birth, subject to partial divestment by the birth of later sons. However, the case law on this point is sparse.

b. **Postponed gift to a class (with no condition precedent):** If the class is already closed at the time the postponement ends (e.g., at the end of a present possessory life estate), all members of the class will be included and will take. If the class has members but is not yet closed at the time the postponement ends, all members of the class conceived at the time the postponement ends will be included and may take. However, the class will close to the exclusion of after-born children, who may not take. If the class has no members at the time the postponement ends, all members of the class, whenever born, will be included and may take.

EXAMPLE: T devises "to A for life, remainder to the children of B."

i. If B is dead at the time of T's death, the class of B's children will be closed. Therefore, all of B's children will be included and may take.

ii. If B dies after T but before A, the class of B's children will also be closed. Therefore, all of B's children will be included and may take.

iii. If B is alive at the time of A's death and B has children at that time, all children then born are included and are entitled to distribution at A's death. However, the class will close at that time to the exclusion of after-born children.

iv. If B is alive at A's death but does not have children at that time, no child is then entitled to immediate distribution. The class should remain open. Therefore, all of B's children, whenever born, should be included and should be able to take. Again, some authorities suggest that the first-born child takes the entire estate on her birth, subject to partial divestment by the birth of later children.

c. **Immediate gift to a class coupled with a condition precedent:** An immediate gift to a class may be coupled with a condition precedent. In that case, the class closes when the first member of the class satisfies the condition. All then born members of the class are included and make take if and when they satisfy the condition. However, after-born persons will be excluded.

EXAMPLE: O conveys "to B's children who earn an MBA degree."

i. If B is dead at the time the conveyance is made, the class of B's children will be closed. Therefore, all of B's children will be included and may take, if and when they earn an MBA

ii. If B is alive at the time the conveyance is made, and B has a child who has earned an MBA, the class will close, because that child is entitled to immediate distribution. All of B's then born children will be included, and they may take if and when they earn an MBA However, all after-born children will be excluded.

iii. If B is alive at the time the conveyance is made, and has no children or has children but none has yet earned an MBA, the class will remain open. The class will close if and when a child of B earns an MBA All children of B born at the time the first child earns an MBA will be included, and they may take, if and when they earn an MBA All children born after the first child earns an MBA are excluded.

d. **Gift to a class with a combination of postponements (combined with a condition precedent):** A gift to a class may be made with a combination of postponements (combined with a condition precedent). In such a case, the postponement is deemed to end, and the class closes, when the last condition is satisfied. All members of the class born before the class closes are included and may take, if and when they satisfy the condition. However, all after-born persons are excluded.

EXAMPLE: O conveys "to A for life, remainder to B's children who reach 21."

i. If B is dead at the time the conveyance is made, the class of B's children will be closed. Therefore, all of B's children will be included, and they may take, if and when they reach 21.

ii. If B is alive when the conveyance is made but dies before A, the class of B's children will also be closed. Therefore, all of B's children will be included and they may take, if and when they reach 21.

iii. If B is alive at the time of A's death and B has a child who is 21, that child is entitled to distribution at A's death. Therefore, the class will close at that time. All children born before A's death will be included and may take, if and when they reach 21. However, children born after the class closes will be excluded.

iv. If B is alive at A's death and has no children or has children, none of whom has reached 21, no child is entitled to distribution at A's death (which is the first postponement). Therefore, the class remains open until a child of B reaches 21 (which is the second postponement). When a child of B reaches 21, the class closes. All children conceived at the time a child of B reaches 21 will be included and may take, if and when they reach 21. However, children born after the class closes are excluded.

D. RULE AGAINST PERPETUITIES

1. **Common Law:** The common law Rule Against Perpetuities (RAP) provides that "[n]o interest is good unless it must vest, if at all, not later than twenty-one years after some life in being at the creation of the interest." To determine whether an interest violates the common law RAP, the following steps may be used:

   a. **Interests subject to RAP:** The first step is to identify the interests subject to RAP. The following interests are subject to RAP: options to purchase land not incident to a lease, powers of appointment, rights of first refusal, remainders that are subject to open, contingent remainders, and executory interests. The following interests are not subject to RAP: presently possessory estates, charitable trusts, resulting trusts, reversionary interests, and completely vested remainders.

   b. **Life or lives in being:** The second step is to identify the life or lives in being that may be used as measuring lives. A life in being may, but need not, receive an interest in the document that creates the interest under scrutiny. There is no limit on the number of lives in being, as long as they may be identified by or through the creating document. However, to serve as a measuring life, a life in being must in some way be connected to the vesting of the interest under scrutiny.

      i. **Express life in being:** An express life in being is a person named in the document that creates the interests under consideration. In the grant "O conveys to A for life," O and A are express lives in being.

      ii. **Implied life in being:** An implied life in being is a person who is not named in but may be implied from the document that creates the interests under scrutiny. In the devise "to my grandchildren," the testator's children are implied lives in being.

iii. **Class members as lives in being:** A class cannot be used as measuring lives unless the class is closed at the time the gifts are created.

c. **Timely vesting or failing of interest:** The third step is to determine whether the interests subject to RAP will vest or fail within 21 years of the life or lives in being. Under the common law RAP, interests are analyzed under the "might have been" rule. Under the "might have been" rule, an interest violates RAP if there is any chance, however remote, that the interest might vest more than twenty-one years after a life in being. Under the might have been rule, interests are scrutinized at the time of creation. The time of creation is the date that the creating instrument takes effect. If the interests under scrutiny are created in a deed, the time of creation is the date that the deed is delivered. If the interests under scrutiny are created in a will, the time of creation is the date of the testator's death.

d. **Elimination of void gift:** The fourth and final step is to eliminate the gift that violated RAP. The violating gift is treated as being void ab initio. However, the rest of the gift is left intact.

EXAMPLE: O conveys "to A for so long as liquor is not served on the premises, but if liquor is served, to B." The shifting executory interest in B is void, because it is possible that an heir of A may serve liquor on the premises more than 21 years after the deaths of A and B. Therefore, A is left with a fee simple determinable. O has a possibility of reverter.

EXAMPLE: O conveys "to A, but if liquor is served then to B." Again, the shifting executory interest in B is void. (See the discussion below.) However, when the executory interest is eliminated, A is left with a fee simple absolute. Therefore, O retains nothing.

e. **RAP Examples**

i. **Fertile octogenarian:** O conveys "to A for life, remainder to A's children for life, remainder to A's grandchildren."

(a) **Interests subject to RAP:** A's life estate is presently possessory and therefore is not subject to RAP. Depending on whether A currently has children, the remainder for life in A's children is either contingent or subject to open (because A is conclusively presumed to be capable of having more children) and therefore is subject to RAP. Depending on whether A currently has grandchildren, the remainder is A's grandchildren is either contingent or subject to open and therefore is subject to RAP.

(b) **Life or lives in being:** O and A are express lives in being. Even if children or grandchildren are already born, these persons are members of an open class and therefore cannot serve as lives in being. Therefore O and A are the only possible measuring lives.

(c) **Vesting or failing within 21 years of the life or lives in being:** A's children will take (or not take) at A's death; hence, their interest is valid. However, A's grandchildren may well take more than 21 years after O and A die. Hence, their interest violates RAP.

(d) **Eliminating void gifts:** A retains her life estate. A's children will take for life after A dies. Because the interest in A's grandchildren is void, O retains a reversion, which will fall in after A's children die.

ii. **Unborn widow:** O conveys "to A for life, remainder to A's widow for life, remainder to A's children living at the death of A's widow."

(a) **Interests subject to RAP:** A's life estate is presently possessory and therefore is not subject to RAP. The remainder for life in A's widow is contingent, because a living person cannot have a widow or widower. Therefore, the widow's contingent remainder is subject to RAP. The remainder in A's children living at the death of A's widow is also contingent, because there is a condition precedent to vesting. Therefore, the contingent remainder in A's then living children is subject to RAP.

(b) **Life or lives in being:** O and A are express lives in being. A's widow is not a life in being, because she has not yet been identified. Because their class is open, A's children may not be lives in being, even if some are already born. Therefore O and A are the only possible measuring lives.

(c) **Vesting or failing within 21 years of the life or lives in being:** The widow will take (or not take) at A's death. Hence her interest is valid. However, the children may well take more than 21 years after O and A die. Hence, their interest violates RAP.

(d) **Eliminating void gifts:** A retains his life estate. A's widow will take for life after A dies (if she survives A). Because the interest in A's children is void, O retains a reversion, which will fall in when A's widow dies.

iii. **Charity to charity rule:** O conveys "to A Charity for so long as the premises are used for charitable purposes, but if the premises cease to be used for charitable purposes, then to B Charity." Normally, a shifting executory interest in fee violates RAP, because the executory interest could fall in many years after the deaths of all lives in being at the time the interest was created. However, for policy public reasons, if both A and B are charities, the shifting executory interest in B Charity will be deemed to be valid under RAP.

iv. **Rule of convenience:** O conveys "to such of A's children as shall reach the age of 25."

(a) Assume A is living at the time of this grant and has two children, B, age 26, and C, age 24. Because she is 26, B is entitled to immediate distribution. As a result, the Rule of Convenience will operate to close the class of A's children immediately. All children born or conceived when the class closes (B and C) will be allowed to take upon reaching the age of 25. However, no child conceived and born after the class closes may take, even if the child eventually reaches the age of 25.

(b) Assume that A is alive at the testator's death and has three children, B, age 24, C, age 23, and D, age 19.

   (i) **Interests subject to RAP:** Because no child of A has reached 25, A's children have a springing executory interest, which is subject to RAP.

   (ii) **Life or lives in being:** O and A are express lives in being. The class of A's children remains open, because A is alive, and no child of A is entitled to immediate distribution, because no child of A has reached the age of 25. Therefore, the class of A's children cannot be measuring lives.

   (iii) **Vesting or failing within 21 years of the life or lives in being:** It is possible that a child of A could reach 25 more than 21 years after the deaths of O and A. Therefore, the springing executory interest in the children of A violates RAP.

   (iv) **Eliminating void gifts:** O is left with a fee simple absolute.

2. **Statutory Rule (USRAP):** Some states have adopted statutory revisions of the Rule Against Perpetuities. Under the Uniform Statutory Rule Against Perpetuities, a nonvested interest in real or personal property is invalid unless (1) it satisfies the common law RAP, or (2) it vests or terminates within 90 years of its creation, which is the "wait and see" test. Under the wait and see branch of USRAP, the court waits until the end of the prescribed period to determine whether the interest actually vested or failed within the prescribed period.

EXAMPLE: In 1990, Z conveys "to A for life, remainder to A's children for life, remainder to A's grandchildren." Assume that, at the time the conveyance is made, A is 55 and has one child, B, who is 16. In 1995, B marries. In 2001, a child C, is born to B. A dies in 2004 (at the age of 69). B dies in 2040 (at the age of 66). C may take the property in 2040. The remainder to A's grandchildren would be void under common law RAP. (See the Fertile Octogenarian example above.) However, because C actually takes within 90 years of the conveyance, her interest is valid under USRAP.

V. POWERS OF APPOINTMENT

A. **DEFINITION:** A "power of appointment" is a power created by the donor of the power in the donee of the power, which gives the donee the power to name the person or persons who will take certain property. A power of appointment is personal to the donee. Therefore, the donee may not assign, delegate, or devise the power.

1. **Presently Exercisable:** A power of appointment is presently exercisable if the donee may exercise it during his lifetime. A presently exercisable power of appointment may also be exercised by the donee in his will, unless the donor provided otherwise.

2. **Testamentary:** A power of appointment is testamentary if it is exercisable only by the donee's will.

3. **Relation Back:** Through the doctrine of relation back, an appointment relates back to the date the donor created the power. Therefore, the appointee is deemed to take directly from the donor, not the donee.

B. **DONEE'S RELATIONSHIP TO APPOINTIVE PROPERTY**

1. **Agent of Donor:** In exercising a power of appointment, the donee acts as the agent of the donor. Therefore, the donee is not considered to be the owner of the property that is subject to the power. Generally, the donee's creditors cannot reach the appointive property. However, there are instances in which a creditor of the donee of a general power may reach the appointive property (see below).

2. **Contract to Appoint:** The donee of a testamentary power may not make a contract to appoint. In contrast, the donee of a presently exercisable power may make a contract to appoint. If the subject of the contract is a presently exercisable special power, the contract may provide for the exercise of the power in favor of a non-object of the power.

C. **PARAMETERS OF GENERAL AND SPECIAL POWERS**

1. **General Power of Appointment:** A general power of appointment gives the donee of the power the right to appoint the property to anyone, including the donee. The creditors of a donee of a general power of appointment may reach appointive property if:

    a. The donee exercises the general power; or

    b. The donee is also the donor of the general power.

    In either case, creditors may reach the appointive property even if the power is not exercised. If the donee fails to exercise a general power of appointment:

    a. The property will go to the person designated to receive the gift in default of appointment, if the donor so provided in the instrument creating the power; or

b. In the absence of a gift in default, the property will pass by intestacy if the donor died intestate or through the residuary clause of the donor's will if the donor died testate.

2. **Special Power of Appointment**

   a. **Definition:** A "special power of appointment" gives the donee the right to appoint the property to a limited class of persons (the "objects" of the power).

   b. **Exclusive and nonexclusive special powers of appointment:**

      i. **Exclusive power:** An "exclusive power of appointment" gives the donee the right to exercise the power in favor of some, but not all, of the objects of the power.

      ii. **Nonexclusive power:** A "nonexclusive power of appointment" must be exercised in favor of all objects of the power. If the donee has a nonexclusive special power, the donee may not favor some objects over others. Instead, the donee must appoint a substantial share to all objects.

      iii. **Presumption of exclusive power:** A special power is presumed to be exclusive, unless the donor provided otherwise in the instrument creating the power.

      iv. **Donee's creditors:** The creditors of a donee of a special power may not reach the appointive property; even if:

         (1) The donee exercised the power; or

         (2) The donee is also the donor of the power.

      v. **Failure to exercise power:** If the donee fails to exercise a special power of appointment:

         (1) The property will go to the person designated to receive the gift in default of appointment, if the donor so provided in the instrument creating the power; or

         (2) In the absence of a gift in default, a gift in default of appointment may be implied.

D. **PROCEDURE FOR EXERCISING A POWER OF APPOINTMENT:** Unless the donor provides otherwise, a donee may exercise a power of appointment through any instrument that is capable of transferring title to property. Unless the donor directs otherwise, intent to exercise a power may be demonstrated by the inclusion in a will of a blanket clause, which states that the residue of the testator's estate includes any property over which the testator had a power of appointment. In the absence of a contrary direction from the donor, a court may find that a power of appointment has been exercised by implication, if:

1. The donee attempted to dispose of the appointive property as though he owned it; or

2. The donee's disposition of the appointive property has no meaning, unless it is treated as an exercise of the power.

E. **POWERS OF APPOINTMENT AND THE RULE AGAINST PERPETUITIES:**
The validity of the power of appointment itself, the gifts the power may be used to create, and the gifts made in default of the exercise of the power must be examined under the Rule Against Perpetuities.

1. **Validity of the Power of Appointment**

   a. **Presently exercisable general power of appointment:** A presently exercisable general power of appointment is valid under the Rule Against Perpetuities if it is exercisable within the applicable perpetuities period, measured from the date the power was created.

   b. **Testamentary or special power:** To be valid under the Rule Against Perpetuities, a testamentary or a special power must be exercised within the applicable RAP period, measured from the date the power was created.

2. **Validity of Appointed Interests**

   a. **Interest created by the exercise of a presently exercisable general power:** Under the Rule Against Perpetuities, the validity of an interest created by the exercise of a presently exercisable general power of appointment is measured from the exercise of the power.

   b. **Interest created by the exercise of a testamentary or a special power of appointment:** When an interest is created by the exercise of a testamentary or a special power of appointment, the doctrine of relation back applies. Under that doctrine, the appointment will be read back to the date on which the power was created. Therefore, the perpetuities period commences on the date the power was created. However, circumstances existing on the date the power was exercised will also be taken into account to determine validity of appointment.

3. **Validity of Gift in Default of Appointment**

   a. **Valid power of appointment:** If a valid power of appointment is not exercised by the done, the perpetuities period is measured from the moment the power expires (e.g., when the donee dies), as if the donee made an appointment in terms identical to the gift in default.

   b. **Invalid power of appointment:** If a power of appointment is invalid, power is ignored, and the gift in default of the exercise of the power is analyzed under normal perpetuities rules, without regard to the power.

VI. DISTRIBUTION OF THE TESTATOR'S ESTATE

A. **CLASSIFICATION OF DEVISES:** Traditionally, a devise is a testamentary disposition of real property, a bequest is a testamentary disposition of personal property, and a legacy is a testamentary disposition of money. Today, most jurisdictions use the word "devise" to describe all three types of dispositions. Devises are divided into four main categories: specific, demonstrative, general, and residuary.

1. **Specific Devise:** A specific devise is a gift of identifiable property. The following gifts are examples of specific devises: "Greenacre to X," "my stamp collection to Y," "the 2-karat diamond ring I inherited from Aunt Tillie to Bess," "all my jewelry to Nell," and my "85 Chevrolet to Bill."

2. **General Devise:** A general devise is a gift that does not give specific property, but rather is payable from the general assets of the testator's estate. A gift of "$5,000 to Joe Jones" is a general gift, from the subject is not a specific item. If the testator does not have $5,000 cash in his estate, assets that have not been specifically devised will be sold, and $5,000 from the proceeds of the sale will be distributed to Joe Jones.

   a. **Devise of property never owned by the testator:** If a testator's will devises property that was never owned by the testator, the devise will be treated as a general devise.

      EXAMPLE: T's will leaves, "a 14-karat gold watch to Bill." However, T never owned such an item. The gift should be treated as a general devise.

   b. **Devises of stock:** When corporate stock is devised, the following rules will be considered in determining whether the gift is specific or general.

      i. **Language used:** If a testator devises "all my shares in ABC corporation to my sister," the devise will be deemed specific. If the testator devises "100 shares of ABC corporation to my niece" or "my 100 shares of ABC corporation to my son," the devise is ambiguous. However, some courts may find the latter two devises to be specific, because the language used refers to shares owned by the testator when she executed the will.

      ii. **Nature of corporation:** If the stock has been issued by a closely held corporation, the gift is likely to be considered specific. In addition, when the gift represents a controlling interest in a corporation, the devise is likely to be viewed as *specific,* because the testator probably desired the devisee to manage the corporation's business.

3. **Demonstrative Devise:** A demonstrative devise is a general gift that designates the fund or property from which it is to be paid. If the property designated *is not sufficient* to satisfy the gift, the balance is paid from general assets of the decedent's estate. For abatement purposes, a demonstrative gift is viewed as being (i) specific to the extent of the property designated as the source of the devise, and (ii) general

as to the balance. A gift of "five thousand dollars to Bob, payable from the proceeds of the sale of my IBM stock," is an example of a demonstrative devise.

4. **Residuary Devise:** A residuary devise is a gift of the remaining portion of the testator's estate after all specific, general, and demonstrative gifts, as well as expenses of administration, have been satisfied. "I leave the rest and residue of my estate to Wanda" is an example of a residuary devise.

B. **ADEMPTION BY EXTINCTION:** Under the identity theory, specifically devised is no longer part of the testator's estate at his death, the gift may be extinguished by ademption.

EXAMPLE: T leaves his 14-karat gold watch to X. Subsequently, T pawns the watch. T fails to redeem the watch and the pawnbroker sells it. T later dies. X's gift is adeemed.

1. **Partial Ademption:** An ademption may be complete or partial. To the extent the devised property still belongs to the testator at his death, it is not adeemed.

   EXAMPLE: T's will leaves Blackacre to Jill. Subsequently, T sells 5 acres of this land. The portion of Blackacre that remains of Blackacre at T's death passes to Jill.

2. **Mitigating the Ademption by Extinction Doctrine:** In reaction to the harshness of the result achieved under the identity theory of ademption by extinction, courts have developed several mitigating approaches.

   a. **Construction of gift as general devise:** Some courts construe an ambiguous gift as a general rather than a specific devise.

      EXAMPLE: T's will leaves 100 shares of IBM stock to Bill. At the time T wrote the will, he had 100 shares of IBM stock. However, when T died he owned none. If the court construes the gift of the IBM stock *as a specific devise,* Bill's gift is adeemed by extinction and he will take nothing. However, the court may construe the gift as a general devise that expresses T's desire to give Bill the value of 100 shares of IBM stock. In that case, Bill is entitled to the value of 100 shares of IBM stock at the time of T's death.

   b. **Will speaks at testator's death:** A court may construe a will to speak at the testator's death. Under that construction, property acquired after the execution of the will may substitute for a previously owned asset.

      EXAMPLE: T's will leaves his home on Maple Street to Jane. Subsequently, T sells this residence and purchases another house, also located on Maple Street. The devise is specific. However, the language used accurately describes property that is a part of T's estate at his death. Therefore, Jane may take the new house.

   c. **Focus on testator's intent rather than identity of the item:** Under the modern approach, in determining whether a gift has been adeemed by extinction, a court focuses on the testator's intent rather than on the identity of the item. Under this approach, a gift is adeemed only if the testator intended the will provision to be determined solely on the basis of the property in her estate at the time the will was executed.

EXAMPLE: T's will leaves "My car to my nephew Sam." When T executed his will, he owned a 1980 Ford. T subsequently sold the Ford and purchased a 1989 Volvo, which T still owned at his death. Absent evidence of intent to the contrary, most courts would construe this devise to mean the car owned by T at his death. Therefore, Sam may take the Volvo.

d. **Change in form:** A specific devise may not be adeemed by extinction if the subject matter of the devise has changed insubstantially in form or name.

EXAMPLE: T bequeaths her two-strand pearl necklace to Judy. Subsequently, T has the necklace restrung as one long strand. Later T dies. The change in the necklace is one of form, not substance. Therefore, Judy may take the necklace.

EXAMPLE: Mollie is the sole proprietor of a woman's clothing store, known as "Mollie's Boutique." Mollie devises "Mollie's Boutique" to her niece, Nan. Subsequently, Mollie incorporates her business under the name of "The Dress Shop, Inc." The business has changed in name only. Therefore, Nan may take the boutique.

e. **Statutory exceptions:** The Uniform Probate Code and many states have certain statutory exceptions to the ademption rule. Under these exceptions, a specific devise gets

   (1) any balance of the purchase price (with any security agreement) owing at the testator's death;

   (2) any amount of a condemnation award for the taking of the property unpaid at death;

   (3) any proceeds unpaid at death on fire or casualty insurance or on other recovery for injury to property;

   (4) property owned by the testator at death and acquired as a result of foreclosure (or obtained in lieu of foreclosure) of the security interest for a specifically devised obligation;

   (5) any real property or tangible personal property owned by the testator at death that the testator acquired as a replacement for specifically devised real property or tangible personal property; and

   (6) if property is sold or mortgaged by a conservator for the care of the testator/ward, or if a condemnation award, insurance proceeds or recovery for injury to property are paid to the conservator or agent, a general pecuniary devise equal to the net sale price, the amount of the unpaid loan, the condemnation award, the insurance proceeds or the recovery. In addition, a devise may receive a pecuniary devise equal to the value of other specifically devised property disposed of during the testator's

lifetime, but only to the extent that the testator did not intend ademption or ademption would be inconsistent with the testator's plan of distribution. U.P.C. § 2-606.

C. **ACCESSIONS:** Additions or changes to devised securities may occur during the time between the execution of the will and the death of the testator. Under the Uniform Probate Code, if a testator makes a general or a specific devise of stock, in addition to the stock remaining at the time of the testator's death, the devisee will receive additional stock acquired by a stock split or a stock dividend. U.P.C. § 2-605. A devisee will also receive stock acquired through mergers or consolidations. However, the devisee will not receive cash dividends paid on the stock before the death of the testator.

D. **SATISFACTION OF DEVISES:** Under the Uniform Probate Code, if a testator makes a gift to a will beneficiary during the testator's lifetime, the gift may be considered to be in whole or partial satisfaction of the testate gift if the inter vivos gift falls into any one of the following three categories: (1) The testator's will provides that the inter vivos gift satisfies the devise; (2) the inter vivos gift is accompanied by a writing that confirms that the inter vivos gift is intended to be in satisfaction of the testamentary devise; or (3) the recipient of the inter vivos gift acknowledges in writing that the gift was made in satisfaction of the testamentary devise. U.P.C. § 2-609.

Valuation of Gift in Satisfaction of Devise: For the purposes of determining satisfaction of a devise, an inter vivos gift is valued at the date the beneficiary comes into possession or enjoyment of the gift or the date the testator dies, whichever occurs first.

E. **ABATEMENT:** Gifts in a will must abate when the decedent made no provision regarding payment of claims or the assets of the estate are not sufficient to pay all of the deceased's debts and also satisfy all the specific and general devises, bequests, and legacies in the will.

1. **General Rule:** Subject to the special abatement rules for omitted spouses and children, or a testamentary directive to the contrary, testamentary devises, bequests, and legacies abate in the following order:

    a. Property passing by intestacy,

    b. Residuary gifts,

    c. General gifts,

    d. Specific gifts.

    Within each class, the shares of a devisee abate pro rata. Gifts of annuities and demonstrative gifts are treated as specific gifts to the extent they are satisfied from the fund or property specified in the gift, and they are treated as general gifts to the extent they are satisfied from property other than the fund or property specified in the gift.

EXAMPLE: T leaves an estate consisting of Blackacre (worth $50,000) and $25,000 in cash. Under T's will, Blackacre is devised to Joe, and the balance of T's estate passes to Martha. T's estate is subject to $15,000 in debts. The debts will be paid first from the residue, which abates before the specific devise of Blackacre. Because the residue is sufficient to cover the full amount of the debt, the devise of Blackacre will not abate. Therefore, Martha will receive $10,000, which is the portion of the cash remaining after payment of the debts, and Joe will receive Blackacre.

F. **EXONERATION:** Under the common law, if devised property was encumbered by a lien at the time of the testator's death, the lien was subject to exoneration. Exoneration requires satisfaction of the lien from residuary assets of the probate estate. However, under the Uniform Probate Code, devises are not subject to exoneration unless the will expressly provides for exoneration. The requisite intent is not demonstrated if the will merely directs the payment of all debts. U.P.C. § 2-607.

G. **LAPSE**

1. **Definition of Lapse:** A testamentary gift may lapse if the beneficiary predeceases the testator. Traditionally, the term "lapsed" was used to describe a case in which the beneficiary was alive at the execution of the will but predeceased the testator. If the beneficiary was not alive at the time the will was executed, the gift was deemed to be void. The typical wills antilapse statute applies to both lapsed and void gifts. A gift may also be treated as lapsed if the beneficiary disclaims the gift.

2. **Antilapse Statute:** Most jurisdictions have adopted an anti lapse statute. Under the Uniform Probate Code and antilapse statutes in most states, unless the will provides otherwise, a deceased beneficiary's gift will not lapse if (1) the beneficiary is a relative of the testator and (2) the beneficiary is survived by lineal descendants. See U.P.C. § 2-603. The U.P.C. and some state statutes require the beneficiary to be a grandparent or a lineal descendant of a grandparent. U.P.C. § 2-603(b). For the purposes of the typical antilapse statute, an adopted child is considered to be a lineal descendant of the adoptive parents. The U.P.C. also protects stepchildren. If a gift does not lapse, it will pass by representation to the surviving lineal descendants of the deceased beneficiary.

3. **Consequences of Lapsed Gifts that are not Subject to the Antilapse Provision:** If a devise fails, the property devised becomes a part of the residue or passes by intestacy if the will does not have a residuary clause.

EXAMPLE: T devises Blackacre to his brother, Bob. Bob predeceases T, survived by two children. Under Bob's will, his entire estate passes to his sister Jane. Because Bob was a descendant of T's grandparents, the typical antilapse statute will protect his gift. Therefore, Blackacre will pass to his children, who are his surviving lineal descendants. Jane will take nothing under Bob's will.

EXAMPLE: T devises Blackacre to his best friend, Mike. Mike predeceases T, survived by his son. Because Mike was not related to T, the typical antilapse statute will not protect his gift. Thus, Blackacre passes under the residuary clause of T's will (or by intestacy if there is no residuary clause).

4. **Survivorship Language:** A testator may include in his will a gift to a person "if she survives me." A court may interpret that language to mean that the testator did not want the antilapse statute to be applied to the gift. However, under the Uniform Probate Code, the antilapse statute will apply unless the survivorship language is accompanied by additional proof that the testator did not want the antilapse statute to apply. U.P.C. § 2-603(b)(3).

5. **Substitute Gifts:** A will may provide for a substitute gift if the beneficiary predeceases the testator. For example, a testator may devise Blackacre "to my daughter Mary if she survives me, and if she does not, to my son John." If the primary taker predeceases the testator but the alternative taker survives the testator, the antilapse statute likely will not apply. If both takers predecease the testator, the courts are split on whether the antilapse statute should be applied. The Uniform Probate Code antilapse statute does apply if both takers predecease the testator. U.P.C. § 2-603(b)(4).

6. **Class Gifts:** If a testator intends that a group of persons shares a devise, the property to be distributed to the devisees may be a class gift. In determining if the testator intended a devise to be a class gift, two factors are frequently considered: (1) whether the testator appeared to be "group-minded," and (2) whether the number of devisees was subject to variance. Subject to application of the anti lapse statute or any contrary intention expressed by the testator in the will, if a devise is a class gift and one of the members dies, his share is divided among the remaining class members.

   a. **Testator's "group-mindedness":** Group-mindedness may be demonstrated by a gift to a group of recipients who are not named as individuals. Often, the members of the group are related to the testator in the same degree of consanguinity. For example, a gift may be made to "my nieces and nephews."

      EXAMPLE: T leaves the residue of her estate to, "my nieces, Mary, Alice, and Lois." Subsequently, one of T's sisters gives birth to another niece, Anne. There is a division of authority as to the testator's likely intent when a gift (i) refers to a group (e.g., "nieces"), **and** (ii) identifies the members of that group by name. If T's devise is viewed as a class gift, Anne receives one-fourth of T's residuary devise. However, if this clause did not create a class gift, Anne receives nothing under the residuary clause of T's will.

   b. **Variance:** If the testator contemplated that the composition or number of devisees could vary between the execution of the will and the testator's death, a class gift will probably be found.

      EXAMPLE: The residuary clause in T's will leaves the residue of her estate to "my grandchildren who are alive at the time of my death." This is probably a class gift. T appears to have been group-minded in making the gift and has written this provision in a manner that indicates that she contemplated that the total number of devisees could vary.

EXAMPLE: T's will leaves the residue of her estate to "my sisters." When T wrote the will, she had two living sisters Ann and Bessie. Ann predeceases T. Ann has a son, Steve, who survives T. Under the antilapse statute, Steve will substitute for Ann, even if the residuary devise is held to be a class gift. Consequently, Bessie and Steve will share the residue equally.

   c. **Adopted persons as members of class:** Unless otherwise provided in the will, adopted persons are deemed to be members of the relevant class.

   d. **When class determined:** In the absence of a contrary provision in the will:

      i. A devise of a present interest to a class includes all persons answering the class description at the testator's death, and

      ii. A person conceived before, but born after, the testator's death or the time of enjoyment, may take if she answers the class description.

   e. **Application of antilapse provision to person deceased when will was executed:** In some jurisdictions, the antilapse statute does not apply to a devisee who was deceased when the will was executed. However, the Uniform Probate Code's antilapse provisions do apply to a devisee who died before the execution of the will. U.P.C. § 2-603(b)(2).

H. SLAYER STATUTES: In most jurisdictions, a person who feloniously and intentionally kills another person, or procures the death of another person, forfeits all death-related benefits that the slayer would have derived from the decedent. These benefits include statutory benefits, including the intestate share, the elective share, the pretermitted spouse or child share, and homestead and other family protections. See U.P.C. § 2-803(b). If the decedent died intestate, the decedent's estate passes as if the killer disclaimed his interest. Thus, a child of the killer may take the killer's share by representation.

EXAMPLE: While driving under the influence of alcohol, H ran into a telephone pole, killing his wife, who was a passenger in the car. Under applicable state law, H is guilty of a felonious homicide for causing the death of another while intoxicated. However, because H *did not intend to kill his wife,* he could inherit under her will or, if she did not have a will, he could take by intestacy.

   1. **Effect of Conviction:** A final criminal conviction of intentional and felonious killing is conclusive for probate purposes. In the absence of such a conviction, whether the killing was intentional and felonious is determined by a preponderance of the evidence. The burden of proof, however, is on the party seeking to establish that the killing was intentional and felonious. The probate court is *not* bound by the results of an acquittal or a plea bargain.

2. **Joint Tenancy:** In most states, when a slayer and his victim held property in a cotenancy with survivorship rights, the slaying results in a severance of the cotenancy. The person responsible for the homicide takes his proportionate interest in the property, and the balance passes as though the slayer had predeceased the victim.

3. **Life Insurance Proceeds:** In most states, the slayer doctrine is also applicable to proceeds derived from a life insurance policy. Thus, where the beneficiary kills the insured in an intentional and felonious manner, the former is deemed to have predeceased the insured.

I.   OMITTED OR PRETERMITTED SPOUSE OR CHILD

1. **Intentional Omission of a Child:** Most states allow parents to exclude their children expressly from testate distribution. However, the testator's intent to exclude his child must be apparent from the face of the will. Extrinsic evidence is generally inadmissible to prove intent to exclude.

2. **Pretermitted or Omitted Child Statute:** Many states have enacted laws that protect children who were accidentally omitted from the will ("pretermitted" children). The Uniform Probate Code also provides protection for a child who has been omitted inadvertently.

   a. Most pretermitted child statutes, and the Uniform Probate Code provision, apply only to children who were born or adopted *after* the execution of the will. A few states, however, extend pretermitted child protection to children who were alive when the will was executed as well as to children who were born or adopted afterwards.

   b. Most pretermitted child statutes *do not apply to grandchildren.* However, some do apply to the children of a testator's deceased child.

   c. **Share of omitted child:** Most pretermitted or omitted child statutes give the after-born or after-adopted child her intestate share, with some exceptions. The Uniform Probate Code provides the following distribution scheme. If the testator had no child living when he executed the will, an omitted after-born or after-adopted child receives a share in the estate equal in value to the share the child would have received if the testator had died intestate, unless the will devised all or substantially all of the estate to the other parent of the omitted child and that other parent survived the testator and was entitled to take under the will. U.P.C. § 2-302(a)(1). If the testator had one or more children living when she executed the will, and the will devised property to one or more of the then-living children, an omitted child's share is taken only from the devises made to the testator's then-living children under the will. In that case, the omitted child receives a percentage equal to what the omitted child would have received if the testator included all omitted children with the children to whom devises were made under the will and had given an equal share of the estate to each child. To satisfy an omitted child's share, devises to the testator's children who were living when the will was executed abate ratably. U.P.C. § 2-302(a)(2). The U.P.C.'s omitted child provisions do not apply if (1) the will shows that the omission was intentional; or (2) the testator provided for the omitted child outside the will with the intent to make a gift in lieu of a testamentary disposition to the child. U.P.C. § 2-302(b).

3. **Pretermitted or Omitted Spouse:** A pretermitted or omitted spouse is a surviving spouse who married a testator after the testator executed his will. Under the Uniform Probate Code and in some states, an omitted surviving spouse may take an intestate share unless (1) the will or other evidence shows that the will was made in contemplation of the testator's marriage to the surviving spouse; (2) the will demonstrates that it is to be effective notwithstanding any subsequent marriage; or (3) competent proof exists that the testator provided for the spouse by transfer outside the will with the intent that the transfer be in lieu of a testamentary provision. U.P.C. § 2-301(a). The omitted spouse's share will be satisfied first from devises made by the testator to the surviving spouse. Next, the share will be taken from other devises, other than a devise to a child of the testator who was born before the testator married the surviving spouse and who is not a child of the surviving spouse. These devises will be exhausted according to the normal rules for abatement of gifts. U.P.C. § 2-301(a).

EXAMPLE: T, a bachelor, made a valid will, leaving his entire estate to his sister, Sara. Subsequently, T married Joan. After the marriage, T executed a codicil that bequeathed his baseball cards to Bart. In some jurisdictions, the republication may cause Joan to cease to be an omitted spouse.

However, courts in other jurisdictions may, in the exercise of their discretion, decline to apply the republication doctrine if the application would deprive the spouse of needed protection or would cause a result that is contrary to the testator's intent. In those jurisdictions, the spouse would continue to enjoy the benefit of the pretermitted spouse election.

4. **Elective Share:** Most states protect the surviving spouse by allowing him or her to elect to take against a will executed by his or her deceased spouse.

   a. **Amount of elective share:** The 1990 version of the Uniform Probate Code gave the surviving spouse the right to take a percentage of the augmented estate, which increased with the number of years in the marriage. The percentage rose from nothing for a marriage lasting less than one year to 50% for a marriage lasting 15 years or more. 1990 U.P.C. § 2-202(a). Under the 2008 revisions to the U.P.C., the surviving spouse may elect to take 50% of the marital-property portion of the augmented estate. 2008 Revised U.P.C. § 2-202(a). The marital-property portion of the augmented estate is determined by a graduated scale, starting at 6% for a marriage of one year and rising to 100% after 15 years of marriage. Revised U.P.C. § 2-203(b). A minimum of $75,000 ($50,000 under the 1990 U.P.C.) is set for the elective share. 2008 Revised U.P.C. § 2-202(b).

b. **Augmented estate:** Currently, the augmented estate is comprised of the value of assets from the married couple's combined estate, which are grouped into four categories.

    i. **Net probate estate:** First, the augmented estate includes the decedent's net probate estate, less funeral and administration expenses, homestead allowance, family allowances, exempt property, and enforceable claims against the estate. 1990 U.P.C. § 2-204.

    ii. **Nonprobate transfers to third persons:** Second, the augmented estate also includes property transferred by the decedent to third persons in inter vivos will substitutes. This category is comprised of (1) property transferred by the decedent during marriage and during the two-year period next preceding the decedent's death; (2) property transferred irrevocably during the marriage in which the decedent retained an interest and property in which the decedent created a power exercisable by or for the decedent or the decedent's estate; and (3) property owned by the decedent immediately before death that passed outside probate. Property passing outside probate includes (1) property over which the decedent was the sole owner, immediately before his death, of a presently exercisable general power of appointment; (2) the decedent's interest in survivorship cotenancies; (3) the decedent's interest in payable on death ("P.O.D.") or transferable on death ("T.O.D.") accounts or securities or Totten trusts; and (4) proceeds of life insurance policies on the decedent if the decedent owned the policy immediately before his death. 1990 U.P.C. § 2-205. The value of property is excluded from the decedent's nonprobate transfers to others (i) to the extent the decedent received consideration for the transfer or (ii) if the property was transferred with the written consent by or joinder of the surviving spouse. 1990 U.P.C. § 2-208.

    iii. **Nonprobate transfers to the spouse:** Third, the augmented estate includes inter vivos will substitute transfers of the types described above that were made by the decedent to the surviving spouse. 1990 U.P.C. § 2-206.

    iv. **Spouse's property and nonprobate transfers:** Fourth, the augmented estate includes the value of property owned by the surviving spouse at the decedent's death, plus amounts that would have been included in the surviving spouse's nonprobate transfers to others if the spouse had been the decedent, reduced by enforceable claims against the property or the spouse. 1990 U.P.C. § 2-207.

c. **Satisfaction of elective share:** The elective share is satisfied first from all interests that pass or have passed to the surviving spouse by testate or intestate succession, plus the value of the decedent's nonprobate transfers to the surviving spouse and the marital-property portion of amounts included in the augmented estate. 1990 U.P.C. § 2-209(a). If those interests are not sufficient, the elective share is then satisfied proportionally first, from third party beneficiaries of testamentary gifts and will substitutes, and second, from third persons who took irrevocable gifts from the decedent within two years of the decedent's death. 1990 U.P.C. § 2-209(b).

d. **Effect of election on other interests:** The elective share is in addition to the spouse's right to exempt property, family allowance, and homestead. 2008 Revised U.P.C. § 2-202(c).

e. **Who may elect:** The election may be made by (1) the surviving spouse, or (2) the surviving spouse's attorney in fact or the guardian of the surviving spouse's property. In all cases, the surviving spouse must be alive at the time the election is made. 1990 U.P.C. § 2-212(a). If the election is made by a conservator on behalf of an incapacitated surviving spouse, elective share funds taken from the decedent spouse's estate and from recipient of nonprobate transfers from the decedent spouse must be placed in trust for the support of the surviving spouse. When the surviving spouse dies, funds remaining in that trust must be returned to the decedent spouse's estate for distribution under the decedent spouse's will. 1990 U.P.C. § 2-212(b).

f. **Time for election:** The election must be made within nine months after the date of the decedent's death or within six months after the probate of the decedent's will, whichever is later. 1990 U.P.C. § 2-211(a). The person making the election may petition the court for an extension, which the court may in its discretion grant. 1990 U.P.C. § 2-211(b).

g. **Waiver of elective share:** The right of election may be waived in writing before or after marriage. 1990 U.P.C. § 2-213.

(i) **Community property states:** Community property states, which automatically give one spouse's property to the other spouse at death, do not have elective share statutes. Instead, each spouse is given one-half of the community property, without a survival requirement. The surviving spouse may take both his one-half share and any portion of the community property the predeceasing spouse devises to the surviving spouse in his will. However, when a testator purports to devise all of the couple's community property rather than the testator's half, the surviving spouse has two options. First, she may choose to take the one-half of the community property to which she is rightfully entitled. However, if the surviving spouse chooses this option, she waives all testamentary gifts. Second, the surviving spouse may take under the will. If she chooses this second option, she waives her community property rights.

5. **Other Family Protections:** Most jurisdictions provide some or all of the following additional protections for the family.

a. **Homestead:** Some jurisdictions provide protection for real property that is considered the homestead of the decedent and her family. To qualify as homestead, property must be owned by a natural person and must be the permanent residence of the owner or his family. Homestead protection may extend to a certain monetary level or a certain acreage. Under the 2008 revisions to the U.P.C., the spouse, or minor and dependent children if the spouse does not survive the decedent, receive a homestead allowance of $22,500. 2008 revised U.P.C. § 2-402. Homestead property is exempt from the claims of most creditors, except those that grow directly out of the property, such as mortgages, real property taxes, and mechanic's liens. The protection from creditors' claims generally inures to the benefit of the decedent's surviving spouse, devisee, or heirs. In addition, restrictions may be placed on the ability of the owner to devise homestead property to persons other than the surviving spouse, particularly if the decedent is survived by minor children.

    b. **Family allowance:** The Uniform Probate Code and most jurisdictions provide a family allowance, which may be claimed by the surviving spouse and minor and dependent children. Under the U.P.C., the allowance must be "reasonable" and may not exceed $18,000. U.P.C. § 2-404. Unless the will provides otherwise, the family allowance is in addition to the spouse or heir's share of the decedent's estate.

    c. **Exempt personal property:** The Uniform Probate Code and most jurisdictions also provide for the spouse, or children if the spouse does not survive the decedent, by protecting certain exempt personal property. Exempt personal property typically includes household furniture, automobiles, furnishings, appliances, and personal effects. See 2008 revised U.P.C. § 2-403. Under the U.P.C., the value of exempt property may not exceed $15,000.

6. **Waiver of Statutory Spousal Protections:** A spouse may waive the right to receive (1) an intestate, elective, or pretermitted share, and (2) homestead protection, exempt property, and family allowance, and (3) the right to be given preference in the selection of the personal representative. A waiver of statutory spousal protections must be in writing. See U.P.C. § 2-313.

VII. WILL SUBSTITUTES

Will substitutes are vehicles used by property owners to make testamentary-like transfer property interests outside the probate process.

A. **JOINT TENANCIES AND TENANCIES BY THE ENTIRETY:** Because they carry a right of survivorship, joint tenancies and tenancies by the entirety are often used as will substitutes.

B. BANK AND SECURITIES ACCOUNTS

1. **Totten Trusts and Joint Bank and Securities Accounts**

   a. **Totten trusts:** A Totten trust is created when a depositor opens a bank account in the name of another person. For example, Darian may open a bank account, using the following language: "Darian Depositor, trustee for Belinda Beneficiary." In a Totten trust, the depositor retains the passbook to the account, and he may make deposits to and withdrawals from the account during his lifetime. Because the depositor is deemed to be the owner of all funds in the account, the depositor's creditors may reach the funds in the account. The beneficiary has no right to the funds in the account during the depositor's life. However, the beneficiary will receive the funds, if any, left in the account at the depositor's death. A depositor may revoke a Totten trust during her lifetime, by withdrawing all the funds in the account or by doing some other act that manifests her intent to revoke the trust. A depositor may also use his will to revoke a Totten trust at his death by leaving the account balance to another person. In addition, a Totten trust terminates if the beneficiary predeceases the depositor.

   b. **Joint tenancy bank account:** Two or more persons may open a joint tenancy bank account. During the joint lives of the owners of a joint account, each joint tenant holds a present right in the funds deposited in the account. On the death of one of the joint tenants, the survivor takes the sum remaining in the account. A true joint tenancy bank account may not be revoked by will.

   c. **"Pay on death" bank account, "in trust for" account, and "transfer on death" securities account.**

      i. **POD bank account:** A person may create a "pay on death" (POD) bank account by opening and funding a bank account with a financial institution. At the time the account is opened, the owner designates a person or persons who are to receive the account assets on the death of the owner.

      ii. **"ITF" account:** An "in trust for" (ITF) account also includes a pay on death designation. Therefore, an ITF account is subject to the rules that govern a POD account.

      iii. **TOD securities account:** A person may create a "transfer on death" (TOD) securities account by opening and funding a securities account with a brokerage institution. At the time the account is opened, the owner designates a person or persons who are to receive the account assets on the death of the owner.

   In each of these accounts, the account owner has the present right to all funds deposited in the account. During her lifetime, the owner retains the right to add or remove funds from the account, to add or remove beneficiaries from the account, and to close the account. The beneficiary of the account has no right to the funds in the account until the owner dies. The account is not subject to probate if a beneficiary survives the owner. However, if no beneficiary survives the owner, the account balance becomes part of the probate estate when the owner dies.

    d. **Convenience bank account:** A convenience bank account is created when a person is given the right to draw, for limited purposes, on an account owned by another person. The person who creates a convenience account has the present right to all sums deposited in the account. The other party may draw on the account presently to pay the owner's bills. However, the other party has no survivorship rights.

C. LIFE INSURANCE POLICIES: A life insurance policy is a contract under which an insurance company promises to pay a sum of money to a named person on the death of the insured person.

    1. **Types of Policies:** The whole life and term life insurance policies are often used as will substitutes.

        a. **Whole life insurance policy:** A whole life insurance policy remains in effect for the life of the insured. In most cases, premiums must be paid annually. When the insured dies, the death benefit will be paid to the beneficiary named in the policy. A whole life insurance policy generally carries a "cash surrender value," which represents the value of the policy during the lifetime of the insured. The cash surrender value is usually smaller than the face value of the policy, which is payable on the death of the insured.

        b. **Term life insurance policy:** A term life insurance policy covers the insured for a limited period of time. After that period, the insured may terminate the policy or may keep the policy and pay premiums that increase annually. If the insured dies during the term, the death benefit is paid to the beneficiary named in the policy. A term life insurance policy does not have a cash surrender value.

D. GIFT CAUSA MORTIS: A gift causa mortis is a gift of personal property made by a person in anticipation of impending death. The gift is conditioned on the donor dying as anticipated, leaving the donee surviving him. A gift causa mortis must (1) satisfy the traditional elements for an inter vivos gift, which are present donative intent, delivery; and acceptance; and (2) be made in contemplation of the donor's imminent death. A gift causa mortis may be revoked by the donor any time during his lifetime. It is also revoked by operation of law if the donor does not die from the peril anticipated by the donor.

VIII. INTESTATE DISTRIBUTION

A. DEFINITION: Intestate distribution laws are applied *when a person dies without a valid will.* Intestate distribution statutes vary from state to state.

B. **SPOUSE'S SHARE:** In most states, when a decedent is survived by a spouse and children, the spouse takes between one-third and one-half of the estate. In most jurisdictions, if the surviving children are all children of the testator's marriage to the surviving spouse, the spouse will take a sum of money in addition to the percentage of the estate described above. Under the 2008 revisions to the Uniform Probate Code, the surviving spouse receives the entire intestate estate if (1) the decedent is not survived by a descendant or a parent; or (2) all of the decedent's surviving descendants are also descendants of the surviving spouse and there is no other descendant of the surviving spouse who survives the decedent. If the decedent is survived by a parent but not a descendant, the surviving spouse receives the first $300,000, plus three-fourths of any balance of the intestate estate. If all of the decedent's surviving descendants are also descendants of the surviving spouse and the surviving spouse has one or more surviving descendants who are not descendants of the decedent, the surviving spouse receives the first $225,000, plus one-half of any balance of the intestate estate. If one or more of the decedent's surviving descendants are not descendants of the surviving spouse, the spouse receives the first $150,000, plus one-half of any balance of the intestate estate. 2008 revised U.P.C. § 2-102. When there are no children, the spouse takes all of the estate. Under the 2008 revisions to the Uniform Probate Code, the surviving spouse also takes the entire estate if (1) the decedent is not survived by descendants or a parent; or (2) all of the decedent's surviving descendants are also descendants of the surviving spouse and there is no other descendant of the surviving spouse who survives the decedent. 2008 U.P.C. § 2-102(1).

C. **CHILDREN AND OTHER DESCENDANTS:** In most states, any portion of the decedent's estate that is not distributed to the spouse, goes to the decedent's children and lineal descendants. Lineal descendants include adopted children and children who are conceived before but are not born until after the death of the decedent. See the discussion below for the rules governing inheritance by and through adopted children. When the decedent had children who predeceased him, and when these deceased children had surviving children, descent will be determined by one of the following three methods:

1. **Strict per Stirpes:** When descent is determined by strict per stirpes, lineal descendants of a deceased person may by representation take the intestate share that the deceased person would have received if she had survived the decedent. Under strict per stirpes, the estate is divided into shares at the "root" generation, which is the first generation after the decedent. Each member receives a share, whether the member is living or dead at the time of the decedent's death. If a member of the root generation predeceased the decedent, the deceased member's share descends per stirpes to the lineal descendants of the deceased member.

2. **Per Capita with Representation:** Under per capita with representation, the estate is divided into as many equal shares as there are (i) surviving descendants in the generation nearest to the decedent that contains one or more surviving descendants and (ii) deceased descendants in the same generation who left surviving descen-

dants, if any. Each surviving descendant in the nearest generation is allocated one share. If a member of the nearest generation predeceased the decedent, the deceased member's share descends per stirpes to the lineal descendants of the deceased member. 1969 U.P.C. § 2-106(b).

3. **Per Capita at Each Generation:** Under per capita at each generation, the estate is divided into as many equal shares as there are (i) surviving descendants in the generation nearest to the decedent that contains one or more surviving descendants and (ii) deceased descendants in the same generation who left surviving descendants, if any. Each surviving descendant in the nearest generation is allocated one share. The remaining shares, if any, are combined and then divided in the same manner among the surviving descendants of the deceased descendants as if the surviving descendants who were allocated a share and their surviving descendants had predeceased the decedent. 1990 U.P.C. § 2-106(b).

EXAMPLE: Dan died intestate. Dan had three children, Ann, Ben, and Carol. Ann predeceased Dan, survived by two children, Ed and Fran. Ben also predeceased Dan, survived by one grandchild, Harry, who was the son of Ben's only child, Gino, who predeceased Dan. Carol predeceased Dan, survived by two grandchildren, Jill and Karl, who were the daughters of Carol's only child, Irene, who also predeceased Dan.

i. **Strict per stirpes:** Dan's estate will be divided into three shares at the root generation, which is his children. Ed and Fran will take Ann's share by representation, Harry will take Ben's share by representation, and Jill and Karl will take Carol's share by representation. The estate will thus be distributed as follows: 1/6 to Ed, 1/6 to Fran, 1/3 to Harry, 1/6 to Jill and 1/6 to Karl.

ii. **Per capita with representation:** Dan's estate will be divided into four shares at the grandchildren's generation, which is the first generation with survivors. Ed and Fran will each take a share in their own right, Harry will take Gino's share by representation, and Jill and Karl will take Irene's share by representation. The estate will thus be distributed as follows: ¼ to Ed, ¼ to Fran, ¼ to Harry, 1/8 to Jill, and 1/8 to Karl.

iii. **Per capita at each generation:** Dan's estate will be divided into four shares at the grandchildren's generation, which is the first generation with survivors. Ed and Fran will each take a share. The remaining two shares will then drop down to the next generation, which is the great-grandchildren. The great-grandchildren will then share those two parts equally. The estates will thus be distributed as follows: ¼ to Ed, ¼ to Fran, 1/6 to Harry, 1/6 to Jill, and 1/6 to Karl.

D. **PARENTS AND COLLATERAL KIN:** In most states, parents of a decedent do not take any share of the estate if the decedent is survived by living children or their descendants. If the decedent is not survived by children or descendants, however, the parents usually inherit the estate.

E. **SIBLINGS OF THE DECEDENT:** A decedent's siblings and their descendants generally will take under an intestate distribution scheme only when the decedent leaves no surviving spouse, children, descendants, or parents.

F. **GRANDPARENTS OF THE DECEDENT:** If a decedent leaves no surviving spouse, children, descendants, parents, siblings, or siblings' descendants, then the estate is divided between the decedent's maternal and paternal grandparents (or their descendants).

G. **OTHER KIN:** Under the Uniform Probate Code and in some jurisdictions, distribution is not permitted to blood relatives who are not grandparents or descendants of the grandparents of the decedent. U.P.C. § 2-103(4). In some jurisdictions, if a decedent leaves no surviving spouse, children, descendants, parents, siblings, siblings' descendants, grandparents, or grandparents' descendants, the estate will be divided as follows: one-half goes to the nearest kin on the decedent's mother's side of the family, and one-half goes to the nearest kin on the decedent's father's side of the family.

H. **KIN OF LAST DECEASED SPOUSE:** In addition, under the 2008 revised U.P.C., if the decedent is not survived by a spouse or grandparents or the descendants thereof, the estate will go to descendants of a deceased spouse of the decedent. 2008 revised U.P.C. § 2-103(b). Some jurisdictions also permit the estate to descend to persons who are grandparents or descendants of grandparents of the last deceased spouse of the decedent.

I. **ESCHEAT:** If a decedent has no surviving relatives of the required degree, his estate will not pass to remote or "laughing" heirs. Instead, the testator's property will escheat to the state.

J. **COMMUNITY PROPERTY STATES:** In some states, property acquired during a marriage is community property of the husband and wife. Property acquired before the marriage or through gift, inheritance, or will is not community property.

1. When the marriage ends through death or divorce and there are no surviving children or descendants, a surviving spouse takes all of the estate.

2. If there is a surviving spouse and surviving children or descendants, there is a split of authority. In some states, the spouse takes all of the estate. In the other states, the decedent's one-half share passes to the children and descendants.

    Under the U.P.C., in a community property state, the surviving spouse takes the entire intestate estate if: (i) no descendant or parent of the decedent survives the decedent; or (ii) all of the decedent's surviving descendants are also descendants of the surviving spouse and there is no other descendant of the surviving spouse who survives the decedent. The surviving spouse takes the first $200,000, plus three-fourths of any balance of the intestate estate, if no descendant of the decedent survives the decedent, but a parent of the decedent survives the decedent. The spouse takes the first $150,000, plus one-half of any balance of the intestate

estate, if all of the decedent's surviving descendants are also descendants of the surviving spouse and the surviving spouse has one or more surviving descendants who are not descendants of the decedent. The spouse takes the first $100,000, plus one-half of any balance of the intestate estate, if one or more of the decedent's surviving descendants are not descendants of the surviving spouse.

IX. CONTRACTS RELATING TO WILLS

A. **CONTRACTS RELATING TO THE DISPOSITION OF A DECEDENT'S ESTATE:** Usually, agreements relating to the disposition of a decedent's estate are made between family members. For example, when each spouse has a child from a former marriage, each spouse may want to be assured that his or her child will be significant beneficiary of the surviving spouse's estate. To accomplish this goal, the spouses may enter into an agreement under which the surviving spouse will receive the entirety of the deceased spouse's estate in consideration for her promise to devise the entirety of her estate in equal shares to the surviving children of both spouses.

1. **Subject to Contract Law:** Agreements pertaining to a testamentary devise are subject to general contract law principles. Thus, an agreement to make a will must satisfy the elements for contract formation and is subject to all defenses to formation and enforcement.

2. **Probate of Will:** If the execution of the will breaches a contract to make a will or a testamentary disposition, the will nevertheless may be admitted to probate. However, the following contractual remedies may be available for breach of the agreement.

3. **Enforcement During Testator's Life:** Ordinarily, there is no action against the testator for breach of contract while he is alive, because an obligation to devise property is not operative until death. However, when the testator repudiates a contract after the promisee has made substantial performance, some courts allow an immediate action for anticipatory breach, permitting legal (and sometimes equitable) remedies.

4. **Enforcement After the Testator's Death:** If the testator dies in breach of the agreement the aggrieved party may (i) assert a breach of contract action against the testator's estate for the value of the property involved, or (ii) seek imposition of a constructive trust in his favor upon the particular property.

B. **JOINT OR MUTUAL WILLS:** Many testamentary contracts involve joint or mutual wills.

1. **Description of Joint and Mutual Wills**

a. **Joint will:** A joint will is a single will that has been validly executed by more than one person. A joint will is admissible to probate on the death of each testator. A joint will ordinarily contains reciprocal provisions (described below).

b. **Mutual wills:** Mutual, or reciprocal, wills are separate documents that contain reciprocal terms. For example, Husband executes a will devising all of his property to Wife if she survives him, and alternatively to their children if she predeceases him. In turn, Wife executes a will devising all of her property to Husband if he survives her, and alternatively to their children if he predeceases her.

2. **No Presumption of Agreement:** The execution of a joint will or of mutual wills generally ***does not create a presumption*** of an agreement not to revoke the will or wills.

   EXAMPLE: T's will leaves all of his property to Ellen, but if Ellen predeceases T, then to the Red Cross. Ellen's will leaves all of her property to T, but if T predeceases her, then to the Red Cross. The reciprocal provisions in these two wills do not create a presumption that T and Ellen made their wills in exchange for the other's promise to make a similar will. Thus, T or Ellen could change his or her will without liability to the other party or potential beneficiaries of the agreement.

X. MISCELLANEOUS CONCEPTS

A. **SIMULTANEOUS DEATH ACT:** Most jurisdictions have adopted a simultaneous death act. This type of statute attempts to resolve title to property when the determination depends on priority of death between two persons and there is insufficient evidence to prove that those persons did not die simultaneously. Under the typical act, if it is not possible to determine which of two persons died first, the property of each person will pass as if that person survived the other person. See U.P.C. § 2-702(a).

1. **Types of Distributions Subject to the Provisions of a Simultaneous Death Act:** The provisions of the Uniform Simultaneous Death Act apply to testate and intestate distributions, joint tenancies and tenancies by the entirety, and life insurance contracts. U.P.C. § 2-702.

2. **Survivorship by 120 Hours:** Under the Uniform Simultaneous Death Act, a person will be deemed to have predeceased the relevant event unless clear and convincing proof is offered that the person survived the event by 120 hours. U.P.C. § 2-702(a) and 2008 revision to U.P.C. § 2-104(a). Under the 2008 revisions to the Uniform Probate Code, the 120-hour survival requirement also applies to homestead and exempt property family protections. 2008 revision to U.P.C. § 2-104(a).

3. **Exception to Applicability of 120-hour Survivorship Rule:** Survival by 120 hours is not required if (1) the governing instrument contains simultaneous death language that is applicable to the case at bar; (2) the governing instrument provides that an individual is not required to survive an event by a specified period or requires the individual to survive the event by a specified period; (3) the imposition of a 120-hour survival requirement would cause a nonvested property interest or a power of appointment to the Statutory Rule Against Perpetuities; or

(4) the application of a 120-hour survival requirement to multiple instruments would cause an unintended failure or duplication of a disposition.

B. INHERITANCE RIGHTS OF CHILDREN AND RELATIVES

1. **Adopted Children**

   a. **Adoptive parents:** The relationship of parent and child is deemed to exist between an adopted person and his or her adoptive parent or parents. Thus, an adopted child has full rights to inherit by, from, and through his adopting parent or parents (and their relatives), and they in turn are able to inherit by, from, and through the adoptee.

   b. **Relationship of natural parents and child after adoption:** In most cases, the legal relationship of parent and child ceases to exist between an adopted person and his or her *natural* parents. However, certain exceptions to this rule are recognized. Under the Uniform Probate Code and in some jurisdictions, adoption of a child by the spouse of a natural parent of the child does not preclude inheritance by or through the natural parent. U.P.C. § 2-114(b). In addition, the U.P.C. and some jurisdictions permit inheritance by and through both the natural and the adoptive parents if the child is adopted by a close relative and/or adopted after the death of both parents may inherit . See 2008 revised U.P.C. § 2-119.

2. **Foster Parents and Stepparents:** There is no legal parent-child relationship between a person and his (1) foster parents, or (2) stepparents. Therefore, they do not inherit by, from, or through one another. However, by statute, some jurisdictions permit a person (and his descendants) to inherit from his stepparents or foster parents if it is established that the foster parent or stepparent would have adopted the person, *but for* a legal barrier (such as, refusal by a natural parent to consent to the adoption). Additionally, in the absence of an adoption, a court may permit inheritance by a foster parent or stepparent by finding an equitable or virtual adoption. Equitable or virtual adoption requires proof of the following: (1) an agreement must have been made between a natural parent (or a person with legal custody) and the adoptive parents, (2) the natural parent(s) must perform by giving up the child, (3) the child must perform by living with the adoptive parents, (4) the adoptive parents must partially perform by taking the child in and treating the child as their own, and (5) the adoptive parents die intestate. The burden of proof in most jurisdictions is clear and convincing evidence.

3. **Posthumous Relatives:** Under the common law and in many states, relatives of the decedent conceived before the decedent's death, but born *thereafter,* inherit as if they had been born during the decedent's lifetime.

   EXAMPLE: T's will leaves the residue of his estate to his grandchildren. When T dies, one of his daughters and her husband had conceived a child, but the child had not yet been born. Because the unborn child was conceived prior to T's death, she will take a share equal to the other grandchildren who were alive when T died.

4. **Half Blood Relatives:** Half blood siblings share one but not both parents. Whole blood siblings have the same mother and father. Under the Uniform Probate Code and in most states, relatives of the half blood inherit as if they were of the whole blood. However, some jurisdictions still follow the traditional common law rule, which distinguishes between whole and half blood relatives when descent is collateral. Under this traditional rule, a half blood sibling will take half as much as a whole blood sibling. However, when descent is lineal, half blood and whole blood siblings take equally.

EXAMPLE: H and his wife W have a child, C. W dies and H marries S. They have two children, A and B. A few years later, B dies intestate, survived only by A and C. Under the U.P.C. and the majority rule, Both A and C inherit equal shares of B's estate. However, under the traditional common law rule, A, as the whole blood sibling, would take twice as much as C, the half blood sibling. As a result, A would take 2/3 of B's estate, and C would take the remaining 1/3.

5. **Nonmarital Children:** In all states, a child born out of wedlock inherits from his mother and his mother's kin, who also inherit from the child. In most states, a child has inheritance rights through his natural father and his father's kin when the father has married the mother, the father has acknowledged the child as his natural offspring, or there has been a judicial determination of paternity. The Uniform Probate Code provides that the marital status of the natural parents has no effect on inheritance rights from and through their child. U.P.C. § 2-114(a). However, parents may not inherit from a child unless they openly recognize and and have not refused to support the child. U.P.C. § 2-114(c).

C. WILL CONTESTS

1. **Standing:** To contest a will, or a portion thereof, a person must be an interested party.

2. **"No Contest" ("in Terrorem") Clauses:** An in terrorem clause provides that a beneficiary will forfeit his gift if he challenges the will. In most states and under the Uniform Probate Code, an in terrorem clause is invalid if a beneficiary challenges the will *in good faith* and *with probable cause* U.P.C.§§ 2-517 and 3-905. In some jurisdictions, if a challenge is baseless, an in terrorem clauses may be enforced. However, in other states, an in terrorem clause is unenforceable in all cases.

D. MORTMAIN STATUTES:
A mortmain statute is legislation that invalidates testamentary gifts to religious institutions. Most states no longer have mortmain statutes. Furthermore, most states do not limit testamentary gifts to charities. However, a few states limit gifts to charities that are contained in a will made within a prescribed period of time preceding the decedent's death.

E. ADVANCEMENTS:
An advancement is a transfer to a potential beneficiary that occurs before the intestate death of the decedent. A transfer will be treated as an advancement if the decedent declared in a contemporaneous writing or the heir acknowledged in writing that the gift is an advancement.

1. **Valuation of Advancement:** If a beneficiary received a cash advancement, the value of the advancement will be set at the sum received. If the beneficiary received an advancement in the form of property, under the Uniform Probate Code, the value of the advancement will be determined by the value of the property at the time the heir took possession of the property or at the time of the decedent's death, whichever occurred first. U.P.C. § 2-109(b).

2. **Hotchpot:** After the court determines that an advancement has been made and the value of the advancement has been set, the court must determine the intestate share of the beneficiary who received the advancement. That determination is made through a common law computation called "hotchpot." Under hotchpot, for computational purposes, the value of the advancement is added back into the value of the decedent's estate. The beneficiary's intestate share of this hotchpot estate is then determined. The value of the advancement is then subtracted from the intestate share of the hotchpot estate, resulting in the actual intestate share.

   Example of Hotchpot. Belinda received an acknowledged advancement of $100,000 from her father. Subsequently, Belinda's father died, leaving an estate of $500,000. Belinda's father was survived by three children, Belinda, Charles, and Dara. To determine the value of Belinda's estate, the following computation is made:

   $500,000 Value of Father's Intestate Estate

   + 100,000 Value of Belinda's Advancement

   600,000 Value of Hotchpot Estate

   × 1/3 Representing Division of Estate into Three Parts

   200,000 Share of Each Beneficiary of Hotchpot Estate

   − 100,000 Value of Belinda's Advancement

   $100,000 Belinda's Intestate Share of Her Father's Estate

F. **DISCLAIMERS:** Under the Uniform Disclaimer of Property Interests Act, a person may disclaim an interest in or power over property. A disclaimer is often made for tax purposes. U.P.C. §-2-1117.

1. **Who may Disclaim:** A disclaimer may be made by an owner of a property interest or a fiduciary of the owner, even if the interest is subject to a spendthrift provision or a restriction on the right to disclaim. § 2-1105(a) and (b).

2. **Type of Interest that may be Disclaimed:** A person may disclaim any type of property interest, including a present estate, a future interest, a survivorship interest in a cotenancy, and a power of appointment. The disclaimed interest may have been created by testate or intestate gift or inter vivos transfer. See U.P.C. §§ 2-1106–2-1111.

3. **Writing Required:** The disclaimer must be made in a writing that is signed by the disclaimant, that is identified as a disclaimer, and that describes the interest

or power that is being disclaimed. U.P.C. § 2-1105(c). The disclaimer must be delivered to the party, such as the personal representative of an estate, that has the duty to distribute the disclaimed interest. U.P.C. § 2-1112. A disclaimer is required to be filed in court only when there is no one to whom delivery can be made. Comment to U.P.C. § 2-1112. To provide constructive notice to subsequent purchasers of disclaimed real property, a disclaimer may be recorded according to state recording law. U.P.C. § 2-1115.

4. **Effective Date of Disclaimer:** In most cases, the disclaimer takes effect when the instrument creating the interest becomes irrevocable. If the interest arose under intestacy, the disclaimer takes effect at the intestate's death. U.P.C. § 2-1106. A disclaimer of a survivorship interest in a cotenancy takes effect at the death of the other cotenant.

   Generally, if a person properly disclaims a property interest, the property will be distributed as if the disclaimant died immediately before the time set for distribution of the interest to the disclaimant. U.P.C. §§ 2-1106.

5. **Limits on Right to Disclaim:** A disclaimer is not permitted if (1) the beneficiary has waived in writing the right to disclaim, (2) the beneficiary has accepted the benefit of gift, (3) the beneficiary has voluntarily assigned, transferred, or encumbered the property, or (4) the property has been sold pursuant to judicial process. U.P.C. § 2-1113.

TRUE-FALSE QUESTION
TOPIC LIST

1. Oral wills

2. Negative bequests

3. "Sound mind" standard

4. Undue influence

5. Severability of will provisions

6. Interested witnesses

7. Extrinsic evidence to show lack of testamentary intent

8. Conditional wills

9. Mistake as to will being signed

10. Mistake as to legal effect of language or law

11. Erroneous description

12. Witness requirements for attested wills

13. Signature requirements for wills

14. Competent witnesses

15. Validity of holographic wills

16. Revocation by subsequent will or codicil

17. Destruction of a will

18. Inadvertently lost wills

19. Revocation of a codicil

20. Effect of revocation of a will on its codicils

21. General vs. specific devises

22. Ademption by extinction

23. Satisfaction

24. Lapsing of gifts

25. Slayer statute

26. Exoneration

27. Enforcement of a contract to make a will

28. Revocation of joint or mutual wills

29. Will contests

30. Simultaneous death act

TRUE-FALSE QUESTIONS

(Circle Correct Answer)

1. **T F** Oral wills are valid in most jurisdictions.

2. **T F** Under the traditional rule, a document that disinherits one or more persons but does not dispose of property is still effective as a will.

3. **T F** To perform a testamentary act, the testator must be of "sound mind." The "sound mind" standard is easier to satisfy than the mental competency required for most other legal acts.

4. **T F** Requesting, suggesting, or advising a change in a testator's will does not constitute undue influence.

5. **T F** If only a particular devise in a will is tainted by improper conduct such as undue influence or duress, the rest of the will may be valid.

6. **T F** In most states, a person may benefit from a will and also be a witness to the will.

7. **T F** Extrinsic evidence is generally admissible to show that a testator lacked testamentary intent.

8. **T F** The effectiveness of a will may be expressly made contingent upon the occurrence or nonoccurrence of a prospective event or condition.

9. **T F** If a person mistakenly signs a will not his own, but the terms of the will signed mirror those of the testator's will, under the modern trend the requisite testamentary intent has been satisfied.

10. **T F** If a testator is mistaken about the legal consequences of his testamentary scheme or the effect of language used in his will, the will is generally invalidated.

11. **T F** If a person or property is inaccurately described in a will, the devise is invalid.

12. **T F** In most states, three witnesses are required for an attested will.

13. **T F** If a testator signs his will using his nickname, the will is ordinarily held to be valid.

14. **T F** If a witness becomes incompetent after he witnesses the will, the attestation is still valid.

15. **T F** In most states, a holographic will is valid if its material portions are in the testator's handwriting.

16. **T F** Even if it does not expressly do so, a subsequent will or codicil may revoke a prior will.

17. **T F** A testator may revoke her will by destroying it.

18. **T F** If a will is inadvertently lost, it is considered to be revoked.

19. **T F** The revocation of a codicil does not revoke the will.

20. **T F** The revocation of a will does not revoke the codicils to the will.

21. **T F** A gift of "$10,000 to Taylor McClennen" would be considered a general bequest.

22. **T F** A specific gift is usually adeemed if its subject matter is no longer part of the testator's estate at his death.

23. **T F** Under the Uniform Probate Code, if a testator devises property to a person and then gives that person the property during her lifetime, the inter vivos gift is treated as a satisfaction if the beneficiary acknowledges the satisfaction in writing.

24. **T F** Under statutory law in most states, if a devisee fails to survive the testator, he does not take his devise under the will.

25. **T F** If a devisee intentionally kills the testator, he may still take under the will.

26. **T F** Under traditional common law, if a specific devise was subject to any mortgage, deed of trust, or other lien existing at the date of the testator's death, the devisee was required to pay the debt himself.

27. **T F** If a testator enters into a contract to make a will, interested parties may sue during his lifetime for enforcement of the contract.

28. **T F** The execution of a joint will or of mutual wills creates a presumption of an agreement not to revoke the will or wills.

29. **T F** A person may contest a will only if he or she is an interested party.

30. **T F** If the inheritance of property depends on priority of death, and it cannot be established by sufficient evidence that one of the persons survived the other, the property of each person shall be distributed, or otherwise dealt with, as if that person had survived the other.

ANSWERS TO TRUE-FALSE QUESTIONS

1. False

Oral wills are generally invalid, except under very limited circumstances. In most jurisdictions, attested wills, or written wills that are witnessed by at least two witnesses, are most likely to be found to be admissible to probate.

2. False

Under the traditional rule, to prevent an heir from taking by intestacy, a testator must make an effective disposition of all of his property to others. Even if it is executed with the requisite capacity, intent, and formalities, a document that merely disinherits one or more persons is ineffective.

3. True

It is easier to satisfy the "sound mind" standard than to satisfy the mental competency standard for most other legal acts. Even persons who have been adjudged to be incompetent to manage their affairs have been held to be of "sound mind" for purposes of making a will or codicil.

4. True

Undue influence requires proof that the testator's free will has been overcome. The testator's free will may be found to have been *overcome* if the testator was susceptible to undue influence, if the ultimate disposition of the testator's estate is unnatural, and if the person who allegedly perpetrated the improper conduct had the opportunity to exert undue influence and was motivated or disposed to do so.

5. True

If only a portion of a will has been tainted, the rest of the will may be admitted to probate. However, if undue influence or duress has affected the testator's overall testamentary scheme, the entire will is a nullity.

6. Mostly false

In some jurisdictions, if a will beneficiary is one of the statutorily required witnesses to an attested will, that person's gift will be void because the beneficiary is an interested witness. However, if the witness is a supernumerary witness, the gift to her may not be void.

7. True

The parol evidence rule does not preclude the introduction of evidence that is inconsistent with a recital that a document is the testator's last will and testament. Extrinsic evidence of the surrounding circumstances and statements made by the purported testator are admissible to show that no testamentary intent was present.

8. **True**

The will's admission to probate is determined by whether the required event or condition occurred.

9. **True**

Under the modern trend, proof may be admitted to show that the writing that was signed did represent the testator's testamentary scheme.

10. **False**

If a testator is incorrect as to the legal consequences of his testamentary scheme or the effect of language used in his will, no relief is granted. Relief is not granted even if the testator relied upon the advice of an attorney in arriving at his erroneous belief.

11. **False**

Under the doctrine of falso demonstratio non nocet (an erroneous description does not invalidate), when the description of a person or property is partially inaccurate, a court may enforce a testamentary gift by excising the superfluous, erroneous language.

12. **False**

In most states, only two witnesses are required for attested wills.

13. **True**

The signature requirement is ordinarily viewed in a liberal manner. Partial names, nicknames, and initials may suffice, provided that the court is satisfied that the testator intended to authenticate the document in this manner.

14. **True**

A person must be legally competent at the time he witnesses a will. To be competent, a witness must have sufficient maturity and mental capacity and must appreciate the significance of witnessing a testamentary disposition. If, however, he subsequently becomes incompetent, the attestation and the will are still valid.

15. **False**

Holographic wills are valid in about one-half of states. In most of these states, the entire will and signature must be in the testator's handwriting.

16. **True**

A subsequent will or codicil may revoke a prior will (or portion thereof) by its express terms or by inconsistency.

17. True

A testator may revoke her will (or a portion thereof) by burning, tearing, cancellation, obliteration, or other means of destruction. The destruction must be accompanied by an intent to revoke the will or portion thereof.

18. False

When there is evidence that the testator's will was inadvertently lost or destroyed, no revocation has occurred. Evidence of the will's provisions is admissible to probate, but there must be sufficient proof of its valid execution and contents.

19. True

The revocation of a codicil does not revoke the will, even if there is extrinsic evidence that the testator intended this result.

20. Usually false

The revocation of a will ordinarily revokes all codicils to that will. However, when codicil is sufficiently complete to constitute a will and the testator intended the codicil to be treated separately, the codicil remains effective.

21. True

A general bequest does not give specific property. Rather, it is payable out of the general assets of the testator's estate. The gift in this question is a general gift because the subject is not a specific item.

22. True

When property that is the subject matter of a specific devise is no longer a part of the testator's estate at his death, the gift is deemed by extinction.

23. True

Under the Uniform Probate Code, if a testator makes a gift to a will beneficiary during the testator's lifetime, the gift may be considered to be in whole or partial satisfaction of the testate gift if the inter vivos gift falls into any one of the following three categories: (1) The testator's will provides that the inter vivos gift satisfies the devise; (2) the inter vivos gift is accompanied by a writing that confirms that the inter vivos gift is intended to be in satisfaction of the testamentary devise; or (3) the recipient of the inter vivos gift acknowledges in writing that the gift was made in satisfaction of the testamentary devise.

24. False

Under traditional common law, the statement would be true. However, most states have passed "antilapse" statutes that allow a substitute taker (usually the devisee's issue) to receive a devise that would otherwise lapse.

25. False

In most states, the killer may not inherit from the decedent. However, the killer's issues generally are not precluded from taking through intestacy, if they are heirs in their own right.

26. False

Under traditional common law, the devisee could demand that the residuary estate satisfy the debt, and the devisee could take free of encumbrance.

27. False

Ordinarily, there is no action against the testator for breach of contract while he is alive, because an obligation to devise property is not operative until his death.

28. False

The execution of a joint will or of mutual wills generally does not create a presumption of an agreement not to revoke the will or wills.

29. True

Only an interested party has standing to contest a will.

30. True

Under the typical simultaneous death act, if the inheritance of property depends on priority of death, and it cannot be established that one person survived the other, the property of each person will be distributed as if that person had survived the other person.

MULTIPLE CHOICE QUESTION
TOPIC LIST

1. Slayer statute/testator's intent

2. Children of slayer

3. Accidental killing of testator/testator's intent

4. Oral wills/testator's intent

5. Intestate succession – spouse

6. Intestate succession – children

7. Intestate succession – parents

8. Simultaneous death

9. Simultaneous death

10. Simultaneous death

11. Effect of divorce on right of ex-spouse to take by testate or intestate succession

12. Requirements for a valid will/holographic will requirements

13. Signature requirements/interested witnesses

14. Interested witnesses

15. Requirements for codicils

16. Ademption by extinction

17. Revocation by later testamentary instrument

18. Advancements and satisfactions

19. Lost wills

20. Sound mind requirement

21. Fraudulent inducement

22. Will contests

23. Uniform Probate Code – intestacy

24. Uniform Probate Code – doctrine of escheat

25. Uniform Probate Code – distribution of the estate

26. Uniform Probate Code – distribution of the estate

27. Uniform Probate Code – distribution of the estate

28. Devises and future interests

29. Restrictions on devised real property

30. Vested remainders

31. Rule in Shelley's Case/Destructibility of contingent remainders/Fee tail

32. Statutory reforms of common law rules

33. Testator's intent

34. Statutory reforms to protect future interests

35. Rule Against Perpetuities

36. Laughing heirs

37. Laughing heirs

38. Anti lapse statutes

39. Vesting of devisee's rights

40. Vesting of devisee's rights

MULTIPLE CHOICE QUESTIONS

Questions 1–3 refer to the following fact pattern.

John, a wealthy New England businessman, makes a will bequeathing a large portion of his money to his only child, Andrew. The will places no conditions on this legacy. However, John hopes that Andrew will use this legacy to start his own business. Andrew, however, would prefer to use the money to travel.

1. Assume for the purposes of this question only that Andrew learns of the provision in his father's will. Andrew decides to murder his father to inherit the money immediately. As his father sleeps one night, Andrew kills his father by shooting him in the head. Will Andrew take his bequest?

   (A) Yes, because his father intended Andrew to receive the money and the testator's intent controls.
   (B) Yes, because Andrew is John's child and may not be excluded from the will.
   (C) No, because Andrew has intentionally killed his father.
   (D) No, because Andrew does not intend to use the money for the purpose desired by his father.

2. Assume for the purposes of this question only that Andrew is barred from taking his bequest because he intentionally killed his father. If Andrew has children, may they take Andrew's bequest?

   (A) Yes, because they should not be punished for their father's act.
   (B) Yes, because grandchildren always inherit from their grandparents.
   (C) No, because Andrew is barred from taking the bequest.
   (D) No, because their father Andrew is still living.

3. Assume for the purposes of this question only that Andrew learns of the money his father plans to leave him in his will.

   Andrew is driving his father to the doctor when he fails to notice a stop sign. His car is struck by a truck, and his father dies instantly. Andrew survives the accident. May Andrew take his legacy?

   (A) Yes, because he did not intend to kill his father.
   (B) Yes, because his father was terminally ill and would have died anyway.
   (C) No, because his negligence caused his father's death.
   (D) No, because Andrew did not intend to use the money for the purpose desired by his father.

Questions 4–7 refer to the following fact pattern.

Recently, Jon promised his friend Sue that he would bequeath to her his vinyl LP collection. Jon also promised Claudia, his child by his wife Wendy, that his will would include a $250,000 legacy for her. In addition, Jon promised Wendy that he would devise Blackacre to her. At that time, Jon was the sole owner of Blackacre.

Shortly after he made these promises, Jon died intestate in a jurisdiction that has adopted the Uniform Probate Code. At his death, Jon was survived by Wendy, Claudia, and Maria, his daughter from a previous marriage. After the payment of debts and costs of administration, Jon's estate included $600,000 in cash and Blackacre, which was worth $725,000.

4. Will Sue receive the LP collection?

   (A) No, if this jurisdiction does not recognize oral wills.
   (B) No, because Jon did not intend for his promises to be enforced.
   (C) Yes, because Jon's promises constitute valid devises.
   (D) Yes, because Jon intended his friends to have the items promised.

5. Will Wendy take sole ownership of Blackacre?

   (A) Yes, because when a decedent dies intestate, the surviving spouse always takes the entire estate.
   (B) Yes, because Jon promised it to her.
   (C) No, because Jon's promise is unenforceable.
   (D) No, because Jon's children are entitled to receive a portion of Jon's intestate estate.

6. May Claudia take the entire $250,000 gift?

   (A) No, because Jon's estate must be divided among Wendy, Claudia, and Maria.
   (B) No, because Wendy will take the whole estate.
   (C) Yes, because her father wanted her to have the money.
   (D) Yes, because Jon's promise was enforceable in most jurisdictions as an oral will.

7. Assume for the purposes of this question only that Jon is also survived by his mother. If Jon's estate passes by intestate succession, may his mother take a portion of his estate?

   (A) Yes, because lineal ascendants may inherit.
   (B) Yes, because she is Jon's mother.
   (C) No, because Wendy, Claudia, and Maria will take the whole estate.
   (D) No, because Wendy will take the entire estate.

Questions 8–11 refer to the following fact pattern.

Christopher and his adult son Sam planned to take a world cruise. Sam is Christopher's son by his first wife, Wanda. Before the two men embarked on the cruise, Christopher made a will leaving all of his property to Sam. Sam also executed a will, which left everything to his friend Sarah.

Both wills met all of the testamentary formalities required by their jurisdictions.

During the cruise, the ship carrying Christopher and Sam sank, killing both Christopher and Sam. Christopher was survived by his second wife, Wilma. Sam was survived by Sarah and his mother, Wanda. The jurisdiction has adopted the Uniform Simultaneous Death Act and the Uniform Probate Code.

8. Who will take Christopher's estate?

   (A) Sarah, because it is presumed that Sam survived Christopher.
   (B) Wanda because it is presumed that Sam survived Christopher.
   (C) Wilma, because it is presumed that Christopher survived Sam.
   (D) The state, under the doctrine of escheat.

9. Who will take Sam's estate?

(A) Sarah.
(B) Wanda.
(C) Wilma.
(D) The state.

10. For the purposes of this question only presume that one of the ship's crew members survived the accident. According to that person, Christopher drowned immediately, but the crew member and Sam floated in the water on life vests for one day after the accident. Unfortunately, approximately thirty hours after the accident, Sam succumbed to exhaustion and died. Who will take Christopher's estate?

(A) Wilma.
(B) Sarah.
(C) Wanda.
(D) The state.

11. What claim does Wanda have to Christopher's estate?

(A) She may claim one-third of estate.
(B) She will inherit anything Sam was to receive under Christopher's will.
(C) She may share Christopher's estate with Sam.
(D) She will take nothing.

Questions 12–15 refer to the following fact pattern.

Lauren and Tom decide to execute wills to provide for the financial security of their 18-year-old daughter, Alison. In particular, they wish to assure that she will have sufficient funds to attend college.

Lauren writes her will entirely in her own handwriting and states that she wishes to leave all of her property to Tom, but if Tom does not survive her, to Alison. Tom drafts a similar will on his computer, leaving all of his property to Lauren, but if she does not survive him, to Alison. Neither will mentions college, but Lauren and Tom both mention to their attorney Steve orally that Alison should use the money for that purpose.

After drafting their wills, Tom and Lauren ask Alison and Steve to witness the wills. All four people sit around Tom and Lauren's dining room table, and Tom and Lauren sign the wills in Alison and Steve's presence. Lauren signs her will with her full name. Tom signs his will "Dad." Alison and Steve then sign the wills as witnesses. Steve then takes the wills for safekeeping. At the time of execution, Tom and Lauren are residents of a jurisdiction that has adopted the Uniform Probate Code.

Eighteen months later, Tom and Lauren are on a plane that crashes over the Pacific. Neither survives. When their belongings are washed into shore, a note is found in Lauren's wallet (in handwriting that is later established to be Lauren's) that she wishes to leave her jewelry to her next-door neighbor, Andrea. The note is neither witnessed nor signed.

12. Is Lauren's January will valid?

(A) Yes, because Lauren wrote the will entirely in her own handwriting.
(B) Yes, but only because it is witnessed by two people.
(C) No, because it is not typewritten.
(D) No, because it is not witnessed by two disinterested witnesses.

13. Is Tom's January will valid?

(A) Yes, because it meets the required formalities for a will.
(B) Yes, because it is typewritten.
(C) No, because Alison is an interested witnesses.
(D) No, because he did not sign his full name.

14. Will Alison be allowed to take under either will?

    (A) No, because she is an interested witness.
    (B) Yes, even though she is an interested witness.
    (C) Yes, because her parents wanted her to have the money.
    (D) No, if she does not go to college.

15. Will the neighbor, Andrea, receive the jewelry?

    (A) Yes, because Lauren clearly wanted her to have it.
    (B) No, because the note was not signed.
    (C) No, because the note was not typed.
    (D) Yes, because the note was adequate to change the terms of Lauren's will.

Questions 16–19 refer to the following fact pattern.

When they were married, Bill and Lori executed wills that left their entire estates to each other. Four years after they executed their first wills, they decided to draft new ones to include their sisters and brothers as well as their daughter Emma who was born after the execution of their first wills. Lori's new will reads as follows:

"I, Lori Testator, being of sound mind, do hereby declare this to be my last will and testament. I hereby leave all of my possessions to my husband, Bill, if he should survive me by 48 hours. If he should not survive me, I hereby devise as follows: I leave my jewelry and $5,000 to my sister, Ruth; my home theater system and $5,000 to my sister, Sarah; my piano to my brother-in-law Chris; and my music collection to my brother-in-law, Steve. The remainder of my estate I devise to my daughter, Emma."

The will is properly signed and witnessed and meets the other testamentary formalities required by the state of their residence.

Bill predeceases Lori, and Lori takes all of Bill's possessions under his will.

16. Assume for the purposes of this question only that Lori needs income and decides to sell the piano. Two years later, Lori dies. Chris makes a claim against Lori's estate for the piano or its value. Will he prevail?

    (A) Yes, Lori's estate will be required to buy back the piano and give it to Chris.
    (B) Yes, Chris will receive the value of the piano.
    (C) No, because Lori no longer owned the piano at her death.
    (D) No, because Chris is Lori's brother-in-law.

17. What is the probable effect of Lori's second will on her first will?

    (A) The second will revokes the first will.
    (B) The second will is treated as a codicil to the first will.
    (C) The second will has no effect on the first will.
    (D) The second will cannot be admitted to probate.

18. Assume for the purposes of this question only that one year after she executes her second will, Lori gives Ruth $4,500.

    If Lori dies subsequently and her second will is admitted to probate, how much will Ruth receive under the will?

    (A) $5,000 and the jewelry.
    (B) $500 and the jewelry.
    (C) Only the jewelry.
    (D) Nothing.

19. Assume for the purposes of this question that Lori executes her second will, then dies several months later. On her death, her will is nowhere to be found. Ruth and Sarah nevertheless wish to have her will entered into probate. Will they be successful?

   (A) No, because the will itself is the best evidence of its contents.
   (B) No, because if the will cannot be found, there is an irrebuttable presumption that Lori revoked it.
   (C) Yes, but they may not testify as to the contents of her will.
   (D) Yes, if they can prove the contents of her will and show that she did not revoke it.

Questions 20–22 refer to the following fact pattern.

Eddie, who has a history of mental illness, executes a will leaving his Rolex watch to his friend Oscar and all of his cash to the charity Mothers Against Drunk Driving (MADD).

The will meets all of the testamentary formalities required by the jurisdiction.

20. If Eddie dies two years from now and he does not revoke his will, will his will be valid and entered to probate?

   (A) No, because of his mental health history.
   (B) No, because he left all of his money to a charity.
   (C) Yes, because he left all of his money to a charity.
   (D) Yes, if Eddie understood that he was making his will and leaving his estate to MADD and Oscar.

21. Assume for purposes of this question only that Oscar has always wanted Eddie's Rolex. Assume also that Eddie intended to leave his entire estate to MADD.

Oscar tells Eddie that MADD has been laundering money. This statement is false, and Oscar knows it, but Eddie believes his friend. Angry at MADD, Eddie executes a will leaving his entire estate to Oscar.

What is the effect of Oscar's deception on the distribution of Eddie's estate?

   (A) The will is invalid, and Eddie's estate passes under the rules of intestate succession.
   (B) MADD will receive Eddie's money, and Oscar will receive Eddie's Rolex watch.
   (C) Oscar will receive the money and the Rolex watch.
   (D) MADD will receive the money and the Rolex watch.

22. Assume for the purposes of this question only that Eddie's will contains a clause stating that anyone who contests the will forfeits his/her legacy. Assume also that Eddie has told Oscar that he plans to leave Oscar his Rolex watch in his will. On Eddie's death, however, Oscar learns that Eddie has left most of his estate, including his Rolex watch to MADD. Eddie has, however, left Oscar his baseball card collection.

Oscar decides to contest the will.

By contesting the will, does Oscar forfeit the baseball cards?

(A) Yes, because he violated the in terrorem clause.

(B) Yes, because Eddie's intent was clear.

(C) No, if he challenged in good faith and with probable cause.

(D) No, because Eddie had told Oscar that Oscar would receive the watch.

Questions 23–27 are based on the following provisions of the Uniform Probate Code:

Section 2-102. Share of the Spouse

The intestate share of a decedent's surviving spouse is:

(1) the entire intestate estate if:

(i) no descendant or parent of the decedent survives the decedent; or

(ii) all of the decedent's surviving descendants are also descendants of the surviving spouse and there is no other descendant of the surviving spouse who survives the decedent;

(2) the first $300,000 plus three-fourths of any balance of the intestate estate, if no descendant of the decedent survives the decedent, but a parent of the decedent survives the decedent;

(3) the first $225,000 plus one-half of any balance of the intestate estate, if all of the decedent's surviving descendants are also descendants of the surviving spouse and the surviving spouse has one or more surviving descendants who are not descendants of the decedent;

(4) the first $150,000 plus one-half of any balance of the intestate estate, if one or more of the decedent's surviving descendants are not descendants of the surviving spouse.

Section 2-103. Share of Heirs other than Surviving Spouse.

Any part of the intestate estate not passing to the decedent's surviving spouse under Section 2-102, or the entire intestate estate if there is no surviving spouse, passes in the following order to the individuals designated below who survive the decedent:

(1) to the decedent's descendants by representation;

(2) if there is no surviving descendant, to the decedent's parents equally if both survive, or to the surviving parent;

(3) if there is no surviving descendant or parent, to the descendants of the decedent's parents or either of them by representation; . . .

Section 2-105. No taker.

If there is no taker under the provisions of this Article, the intestate estate passes to the state.

23. In which situation would § 2-102(2) of the Uniform Probate Code be most relevant to the distribution of the intestate estate?

    (A) Alfred dies intestate survived only by his mother, his granddaughter, and his first cousin.
    (B) Betty dies intestate survived only by her father, her mother, and her first cousin.
    (C) Charlie dies intestate survived only by his widow, his brother, and his aunt.
    (D) Donna dies intestate survived only by her widower, her mother, and her son-in-law.

24. Which of the following is the most convincing explanation for the inclusion of § 2-105 in the Uniform Probate Code?

    (A) The doctrine of escheat is a relic from the medieval world that makes little sense in a modern, industrialized society.
    (B) Distribution of the decedent's property to the state is administratively easier than distribution to the decedent's family.
    (C) Because the decedent is always free to write a will, the distribution scheme is essentially arbitrary, and it makes no difference if the state takes a share.
    (D) The drafters wished to strike a balance between the decedent's probable preference for family members and the desire to preserve administrative convenience.

25. Irving and his first wife (Wanda) had three sons: Tom, Dick, and Harry. Irving and his second wife (Wendy) had four daughters: Dolly, Molly, Polly, and Golly. Dick, Dolly, and Wendy all predeceased Irving. When he died intestate, Irving was survived by Wanda, Tom, Harry, Molly, Polly, Golly, Tom's three children, Dick's one child, Harry's three children, Dolly's three children, Molly's one child, Polly's one child, and Golly's three children. How should Irving's net estate (after payment of debts, taxes, etc.) of $4,200,000 be distributed?

    (A) Wanda receives $2,100,000; Tom, Harry, Molly, Polly, Golly, and Dick's child each receive $300,000; Dolly's three children each receive $100,000.
    (B) Wanda receives $2,100,000; Tom, Harry, and Dick's child each receive $350,000; Molly, Polly, and Golly each receive $262,500; Dolly's three children each receive $87,500.
    (C) Tom, Harry, and Dick's child each receive $700,000; Molly, Polly, and Golly each receive $525,000; Dolly's three children each receive $175,000; Wanda receives nothing.
    (D) Tom, Harry, Molly, Polly, Golly, and Dick's child each receive $600,000; Dolly's three children each receive $200,000; Wanda receives nothing.

26. George died intestate survived only by his father, his widow, his only daughter, his daughter's two children, his late son's three children, and his brother. George's widow was the mother of both George's children and had no other children. Under the Uniform Probate Code, how should George's $650,000 estate be distributed?

    (A) George's daughter and his grandchildren divide the estate equally, each taking one-sixth of the entire estate.
    (B) George's widow receives $350,000; his father receives $150,000; his daughter receives $150,000; each of his daughter's children receives $75,000; each of his late son's children receives $50,000; and his brother receives $150,000.
    (C) George's widow receives $50,000; each of his daughter's children receives $150,000; and each of his late son's children receives $100,000.
    (D) George's widow receives $650,000.

27. Thomas died intestate, survived by his mother, his widow, a son by an earlier marriage, his son's two children, his daughter, and his nephew. The widow was the mother of the daughter and had no other children. Under the Uniform Probate Code, how should Thomas's estate be distributed?

    (A) Thomas's widow receives the entire estate.
    (B) Thomas's widow, children, and grandchildren divide the estate.
    (C) Thomas's widow receives the first $150,000 plus one-half of the estate; his children divide the balance of the estate equally.
    (D) Thomas's widow receives the entire estate.

28. Olivia devised Blackacre "to Allen for life, remainder to Allen's widow for life, remainder to my first child to reach 50." Betty, Olivia's daughter and only surviving relative, bought Allen's interest in Blackacre and has lived there without incident for the last sixteen years. Last month, Allen died, survived by his widow, Wilma. Wilma now claims a life estate in Blackacre and has brought suit to recover the property from Betty who is now 40 years old. Which of the following statutory provisions would have the greatest impact on the result in this suit if it applies?

    (A) The Statutory Rule Against Perpetuities.
    (B) A statute shortening the period for adverse possession from twenty to fifteen years.
    (C) A statute eliminating the doctrine of destructibility of contingent remainders.
    (D) A statute eliminating the Doctrine of Worthier Title.

29. Ophelia devised Blackacre "to Alan and his heirs for as long as alcoholic beverages are not sold on the land; but if alcoholic beverages are not sold on the land, my heirs may reenter and reclaim Blackacre." Alan and his successors have observed the restriction period. However, the city in which Blackacre is located recently announced it is condemning the property to build a new sports stadium. The city will sell beer at the stadium during games.

What is the strongest argument Alan's successors can make to maximize the share of the compensation that they will receive for their interest in Blackacre?

(A) But for the city's action, Alan's successors would have complied with the limitation forever. Thus, the interest in Ophelia's heirs has no value.
(B) By the terms of the grant, Alan's successors may retain the property until it has been used for the sale of alcoholic beverages. It has not yet been so used.
(C) Ophelia's heirs are entitled only to the difference between the fair market value of the fee simple absolute and the fair market value of the defeasible fee.
(D) The restriction on the service of alcohol is an unreasonable restraint. Alan thus had a fee simple absolute, which has passed to his successors.

30. Twenty years ago, Tanya died leaving a will that granted Blackacre "to my son, Sam for life; remainder to the first child of my daughter, Doris, to graduate from medical school." Tanya was survived by two children, Sam and Doris, and by Doris's two daughters, Ann and Betty.

Sam is still alive and healthy. Ann recently graduated from medical school, and now claims a vested remainder in Blackacre. Betty has never applied to medical school. Which of the following additional facts, if true, would most help Ann to establish her claim to a vested remainder?

(A) Blackacre is in a state that recognizes the doctrine of destructibility of contingent remainders.
(B) Tanya knew that Ann's principal goal in life was to become a doctor.
(C) Blackacre is located in a state that recognizes the rule in Shelley's Case.
(D) Doris died shortly after Tanya without having any more children.

31. A common law jurisdiction has enacted statutes that accomplish the following: (i) abolition of the requirement for words of inheritance to create a fee simple, (ii) abolition of the Rule in Shelley's Case, (iii) abolition of the doctrine of destructibility of contingent remainders, and (iv) abolition of the fee tail. Which one of the following grants is most likely to be construed differently in a common law jurisdiction that has not adopted the statutory reforms described above?

(A) "to Beatrice for life, remainder to the first of Beatrice's children to pass a bar examination and that child's heirs."

(B) "to Charlotte for one thousand years if she lives that long, and on Charlotte's death to her heirs."

(C) "to Diana and her heirs on the condition that no alcoholic beverages are sold on the property; but if alcoholic beverages are sold on the property, title shall pass to Edward and his heirs."

(D) "to Faith for life, remainder to George's heirs," when George is the grantor.

32. When Terry died, his will left Blackacre "to Arthur for life, remainder to Arthur's widow for life, remainder to my first child to graduate from an accredited law school." Daphne, Terry's daughter and only surviving relative, had no desire to go to law school, so soon after the will was read she sold her interest in Blackacre "to Arthur and his heirs" for $500. Thereafter, Arthur conveyed his interest in Blackacre "to Boris and his heirs." Last month, Arthur died intestate, survived by his widow, Wilma. She now claims a life estate in Blackacre, and has brought suit to recover the property from Boris. Which of the following statutory provisions would have the greatest impact on the result in this suit if it applies?

(A) The Uniform Statutory Rule Against Perpetuities.

(B) A statute abolishing the Rule in Shelley's Case.

(C) A statute eliminating the doctrine of destructibility of contingent remainders.

(D) A statute eliminating the Doctrine of Worthier Title.

33. Teresa, the owner of Blackacre, has one daughter, Doris. Doris has two sons, Frank and George, by her ex-husband, Harry. Teresa wishes to assure that Harry does not take an interest in Blackacre after Teresa's death. Which of the following clauses best serves Teresa's purpose?

(A) "I leave Blackacre to Doris and her heirs on condition that it never be conveyed to Harry; but if Harry ever acquires title to Blackacre, this devise shall be void and the land shall revert to my estate."

(B) "I give Blackacre to Doris for life, remainder to Frank and George for their lives, remainder to such of my descendants as are living on the death of Harry."

(C) "I leave Blackacre to Doris for life, remainder to Frank and George for their lives, remainder to my heirs."

(D) "I give my daughter, Doris, a life estate in Blackacre, with remainder at her death to my grandsons, Frank and George, share and share alike, or, if either of them be dead, then all to the other."

34. A bill has been introduced into the legislature of a state that still follows the common law rules governing estates and future interests. One section provides:

No future interest shall fail or be defeated by the determination of any precedent estate or interest prior to the happening of the event or contingency on which the future interest is limited to take effect.

Which of the following is the best argument that can be made in favor of this proposed section?

(A) The amendment will make the law in this state the same as in most common law jurisdictions.

(B) The amendment will increase predictability in construing grants containing contingent future interests.

(C) The amendment will promote free alienability of land in this state.

(D) The amendment will better enable courts to give effect to grantors' intentions.

35. In which one of the following cases is there a violation of the common-law Rule Against Perpetuities?

    (A) A devise "to the first of my children to be admitted to the bar," when the testator was survived by three minor children at the time of his death, only one of whom had been alive when the will was executed.

    (B) A devise of Whiteacre "to my eldest descendant then living when the gravel pits on Whiteacre are exhausted," when the testator knew that the gravel pits would be (and they in fact were) exhausted within ten years of his death.

    (C) A grant "to Ally for life, then to Ally's widower for life, and on the death of the survivor of Ally and her widower, to Ally's eldest son and his heirs," when Ally is an unmarried 16-year old-with no children.

    (D) A grant "to Celia for life, remainder to her widower for his life, remainder to Denny for life, remainder to the heirs of Ernie; but if Ernie is still living on the death of the survivor of Celia, her widower, and Denny, then to Ernie and his heirs," when Celia, Denny, and Ernie are the grantor's minor children.

Questions 36 and 37 are based on the following fact situation.

A bill is pending in a state legislature to amend the Probate Code to exclude "laughing heirs." The proposed new section would provide from intestate succession:

If a decedent is not survived by a spouse; issue; a parent or the issue of a parent; or a grandparent or the issue of a grandparent: the intestate real and personal property shall escheat to the State.

36. What is the best argument that can be made in favor of adopting this proposed legislation?

    (A) The proposed legislation should be adopted because in today's society virtually no one would have known his or her "laughing heirs."

    (B) The proposed legislation should be adopted because the expense and difficulty of locating "laughing heirs" outweighs the benefit of including them as heirs.

    (C) The proposed legislation should be adopted because it encourages people to include "laughing heirs" in their wills if they want distant relatives to succeed to their property.

    (D) The proposed legislation should be adopted because it requires a court to distribute the property among the decedent's nearer relatives rather than his or her more distant relatives.

37. What is the best argument that can be made against adopting this proposed legislation?

    (A) The proposed legislation should not be adopted because decedents should retain the freedom to dispose of their property in any way that they choose.
    (B) The proposed legislation should not be adopted because it would interfere with the state's ability to administer escheated property.
    (C) The proposed legislation should not be adopted because most decedents would prefer their property to go to a "laughing heir" rather than to the state.
    (D) The proposed legislation should not be adopted because it does not provide sufficient flexibility for cases in which "laughing heirs" were in fact close to the decedent.

38. Mabel devised Goldenacre to her sister Beth and the rest and residue of her estate to Carl. One year later Beth died intestate and was survived by her son, Sonny, who was her sole heir at law.

    This jurisdiction has the following statute in effect: "If a devisee of a grandparent or lineal descendant of a grandparent is dead at the time of execution of the will, or fails to survive the testator, the issue of the deceased person shall take the decedent's share under the will."

    Mabel died four years later and her will was admitted to probate.

    Is Sonny entitled to receive Goldenacre?

    (A) Yes, because under the antilapse statute, Beth's interest passes to Sonny.
    (B) Yes, because rules relating to lapse do not apply to specific devises.
    (C) No, because intestate succession is inapplicable to devolution of title to specific devisees.
    (D) No, because when Beth died before Mabel, Goldenacre passed to Carl under the residuary clause.

39. Ted devised Blackacre to his daughter Doris. One year later, Ted conveyed Blackacre to Lou. The deed of conveyance was duly recorded. Three years later, Ted died, and his will was admitted into probate. If Doris files suit to quiet title to Blackacre, who will prevail?

    (A) Lou, because he was a bona fide purchaser who paid value.
    (B) Lou, because a prior conveyance effectively revokes the devisee's rights, which can be asserted only after the death of the testator.
    (C) Doris, because a deed is not executed with the testamentary formalities required for the revocation of a will.
    (D) Doris, because the will was executed earlier in time.

40. Davidson drafted a will in which he devised his colonial-style house to his niece Alicia and his personal property to his children, Dwight and Dee.

    Five years later, Davidson purchased a condominium. Davidson furnished the condominium with various items taken from his colonial-style house, including a brick fireplace. Two years later, Davidson died.

    If Alicia brings an appropriate action to have the fireplace returned to her, she should

    (A) lose, because even though the fireplace was a fixture when it was attached to the colonial-style house, it became personalty when it was removed by Davidson.
    (B) lose, because Alicia's right to the house did not vest until Davidson's death.
    (C) win, because the removal of the fixtures diminished the value of Alicia's expectancy in the colonial-style house.
    (D) win, because the fireplace is subject to ademption because it is still part of Davidson's estate.

ANSWERS TO
MULTIPLE CHOICE QUESTIONS

1. (C)

When a devisee intentionally and feloniously kills a testator, the victim's property passes as though the killer had predeceased the victim. Andrew intentionally murdered his father and therefore cannot take under the will. (A) is incorrect because the testator's intent would not control in these circumstances. Murderers cannot profit from their crimes by killing to receive inheritances. (B) is incorrect because in most states testators may choose to omit their children from testate distribution. (D) is incorrect because John's will does not include an express condition on the use of the money.

2. (A)

(A) is the best answer because, in most states, the killer's issue may take the portion that they would have taken under intestacy principles. (B) is incorrect because grandchildren do not always inherit from their grandparents. (C) is incorrect because even if Andrew does not inherit, his children may still take as explained above. (D) is wrong because Andrew's intent is irrelevant.

3. (A)

Involuntary manslaughter does not generally fall under the purview of homicidal devisee statutes. Andrew did not have felonious intent, and he will not be precluded from taking under the will. (B) is incorrect because intent is the relevant factor not the manner of his father's death. (C) is wrong. Although Andrew was careless, he did not intend to kill his father, and his conduct did not rise to the level of recklessness. (D) is incorrect because, absent the use of the money as a provision in the will conditioning, Andrew would be free to use the money as he pleased.

4. (A)

Most jurisdictions do not recognize oral wills, and Jon's statements do not meet any of the testamentary formalities required for wills in most jurisdictions. (B) is incorrect. There is no evidence that Jon did not intend his promises to be enforceable. (C) is wrong, because Jon's oral statements did not satisfy the formalities required for executing a will. (D) is incorrect because absent a formal will, a testator's intent may not be followed.

5. (D)

Under the Uniform Probate Code, when an intestate decedent is survived by a spouse and children, some of whom are not children of the spouse, the spouse receives the first $150,000 plus half of the remaining estate. The decedent's children receive the other half. Jon is survived by a wife and children. Therefore, Wendy will take a portion, not all, of Jon's estate. (A) is incorrect, because Jon's surviving spouse, Wendy will take a portion of Jon's estate. However, it is not clear whether her portion will include Blackacre. (B) is incorrect because

Jon's oral promise is unenforceable as a will. (C) is incorrect. Jon's promise is unenforceable.

6. (A)

Under the Uniform Probate Code, when an intestate decedent is survived by a spouse and children, some of whom are not children of the spouse, the spouse receives the first $150,000 plus half of the remaining estate. The decedent's children receive the other half. (B) is therefore wrong. (C) is wrong because, absent a will, Jon's wishes probably cannot be enforced. (D) is wrong because oral wills are unenforceable in most jurisdictions.

7. (C)

When a person dies intestate and is survived by children or their descendants, his parents do not inherit. Jon's mother therefore has no claim on Jon's estate. Jon's unwritten wishes also have no effect on the intestate distribution of his estate.

8. (C)

Under the Uniform Simultaneous Death Act, when there is insufficient evidence that two parties have died other than simultaneously, the property of each person shall be distributed as if that person had survived the other. Christopher will be presumed to have survived Sam, the sole beneficiary under Christopher's will, is deemed to have predeceased Christopher. Although Sam was a relative of Christopher, Sam was not survived by lineal descendants. As a result, Sam's interest under Christopher's will cannot be protected by an antilapse statute. Therefore, Christopher's estate will pass by intestacy to his second wife Wilma, his sole heir. (B) is wrong because there is no evidence that Sam survived Christopher, so Sam will not take Christopher's estate to pass on to his. (A) is incorrect for the same reason. (D) is incorrect because Christopher's living relatives will take and the doctrine of escheat will not apply.

9. (A)

Because Sam has a will and Sarah is the beneficiary, she will take Sam's estate on his death. (B) would be the correct answer if Sam had died intestate, but he died with a valid will in place. (C) is incorrect. Under a simultaneous death statute, Sam will be presumed to have survived Christopher, and Christopher will not take Sam's estate to pass on to his kin. (D) is incorrect because Sarah will take Sam's estate.

10. (A)

Under the Uniform Probate Code and the Uniform Simultaneous Death Act, a finding of simultaneous death will be made unless one of the decedents survives the other by 120 hours. Sam survived Christopher by only 30 hours. Therefore,

Christopher and Sam will be deemed to have died simultaneously. As a result, Sam may not take under Christopher's will. Because Sam did not leave lineal descendants, his interest in Christopher's will was not protected by an anti-lapse statute. Therefore, Christopher's estate passes by intestacy to his second wife, Wilma.

11. (D)

Divorce usually terminates a former spouse's right to take by testate or intestate succession. Therefore, (A) and (C) are wrong. (B) is incorrect because Sam has a valid will leaving everything to Sarah.

12. (A)

(A) is correct because the Uniform Probate Code recognizes holographic wills. U.P.C. § 2-502(b). (B) is incorrect because a holographic will may, but need not, be witnessed. U.P.C. § 2-502(b). (C) is incorrect. Under the U.P.C., a will may, but need not, be typewritten. U.P.C. § 2-502(b). (D) is incorrect. No witnesses are required for a holographic will.

13. (A)

(A) is the best answer because Tom's will meets all of the required testamentary formalities. It was witnessed by two witnesses, Tom understood that he was signing his will, the witnesses witnessed his signature and were in the same room with one another and with the testators when they witnessed the wills. The fact that Tom signed his will "Dad" does not cause the will to fail, because initials may satisfy the signature requirement. (D) is therefore incorrect. (B) is incorrect. In about half of all jurisdictions, a will does not have to be typewritten to be valid. (C) is incorrect. Under the U.P.C., a person's status as an interested witness has no effect on the validity of the will. U.P.C. § 2-505(b).

14. (B)

Under the U.P.C., a person's status as an interested witness has no effect on the validity of the will. U.P.C. § 2-505(b). Therefore, (B) is correct and (A) is incorrect. (C) is also incorrect. The parents' desire may not be carried out if their wills are not admissible into probate. (D) is incorrect because Alison's parents did not include express provisions in their wills requiring her to use the money for college.

15. (B)

The note will not be considered a codicil because it is neither signed nor witnessed. (D) is therefore incorrect. (A) will not be adequate grounds for considering the note to be a codicil. (C) is incorrect. Even if the jurisdiction recognized holographic wills, the codicil would not be valid because it is not signed.

16. (C)

Because the piano was not in Lori's estate when she died, it is adeemed. Thus, Chris has no claim for the piano or its value. (A) and (B) are therefore wrong. (D) is incorrect. The ademption of the piano gift is not affected by the nature of the relationship between Lori and Chris.

17. (A)

Lori's will does not expressly revoke her first will. However, all of the sections of the second will vary or contradict the earlier will, as the first left all of her estate to her husband and the second leaves her estate to various individuals. Therefore, the second will revokes the first will and is not treated as a codicil. (B) is therefore not the best answer, and (C) is incorrect. Because the will met all of the required testamentary formalities, (D) is incorrect.

18. (A)

The money that Ruth received before Lori's death will not be treated as a satisfaction. Under the U.P.C., a gift to a beneficiary is treated as a satisfaction if the testator so intended it. Because Lori did not indicate that she intended her gift of $4,500 to be treated as a satisfaction, Ruth will take the full $5,000 and the jewlery.

19. (D)

If there is evidence that the testator's will was inadvertently lost or destroyed, no revocation occurs. Evidence of its provisions is admissible to probate, but there must be sufficient proof of its (i) valid execution and (ii) contents. (A) and (B) are wrong. There is generally a presumption that a lost will has been revoked, but that presumption is rebuttable, particularly when there is evidence that the loss was inadvertent. (C) is incorrect because interested parties may testify concerning will contents.

20. (D)

Even if a person has a history of mental health disturbance, he may be considered of sound mind to execute a will. He is competent to make a will or perform any testamentary act if, at that time, he has sufficient mental capacity to be able to (1) understand the nature of the testamentary act, (2) understand and recollect the nature and situation of his property, or (3) remember and understand his relations to his living descendants, spouse, parents, and those whose interests are affected by the will. (A) is therefore incorrect. (B) and (C) are incorrect because most states do not have a mortmain statute that invalidates wills leaving a large portion of an estate to charity. Further, the typical mortmain statute applies only if the gift was made within a limited period before the testator's death. Because Eddie did not die until two years after executing his will, his gift to MADD will not be voided by a mortmain statute, if one exists.

21. (A)

Fraud in the inducement occurs when a testator is deceived with respect to facts on which he relied in making a (i) will, (ii) disposition, or (iii) partial or complete revocation of an earlier will. Oscar fraudulently induced Eddie to leave his estate to Oscar. Therefore, Eddie's will should be declared void. (C) is wrong because Oscar will not be rewarded for his deception. (A) and (D) are wrong because Eddie has not executed a will in favor of MADD.

22. (C)

If Oscar challenges in good faith and with probable cause, he will not forfeit the baseball card collection under the law of most states. Most states will not invalidate the will or penalize a contestor when he acts in good faith and with probable cause. (A) and (B) are therefore incorrect. (D) is incorrect because Eddie's oral statements are unenforceable.

23. (D)

Donna's estate will be divided between her widower and her mother under U.P.C. §§ 2-102(2) and 2-103(2); the son-in-law is not a descendant. Choice (A) is wrong. Section 2-102(2) will not apply to Alfred's estate because he is not survived by a spouse and he is survived by descendants. Choice (B) is wrong. Section 2-102(2) will not apply to Betty's estate because she is not survived by a spouse. Choice (C) is wrong. Section 2-102(2) will not apply to Charlie's estate because he is not survived by a parent.

24. (D)

Section 2-105 excludes the "laughing heirs"—remote family members who were unlikely to have known the decedent. Although most decedents would probably prefer family members (even remote family members) to the state, the preference is presumably not so strong as the preference for closer family members. The difficulty in locating remote family members, on the other hand, is much greater than the difficulty in locating closer family members. Section 2-105 thus strikes a balance. Choice (A) is clearly wrong. Far from rejecting the medieval concept of escheat, § 2-105 codifies it. Choice (B) and choice (C) may be true statements, but they prove too much. Escheat to the state is administratively easier than distribution to close family members, and a decedent is always free to write a will benefiting close family members, but §2-105 only applies to exclude remote family members.

25. (D)

Irving is not survived by a spouse, so UPC § 2-102 does not apply. Thus choice (A) and choice (B) are wrong. The problem is governed by § 2-103(1). The estate is divided into seven equal shares of $600,000—one share for each of Irving's seven children. Thus choices (B) and (C) are wrong. The five surviving children each take their own shares. Dick's one child takes Dick's share and Dolly's three children split Dolly's share; they take by representation under § 2-103(1).

26. (D)

Under § 2-102(1)(B)), the widow receives the entire estate, because the decedent was survived by the widow and descendants who were all also descendants of the widow.

27. (C)

Under § 2-102(4), the spouse receives the first $150,000, plus one-half of the estate. Under § 2-103(1), the children split the other half. The grandchildren get nothing because their mother is still alive. The father gets nothing because § 2-103(2) does not apply when there are surviving descendants. (D) would be the right answer under § 2-102(1(B)) if the widow had been the mother of both of the children.

28. (C)

On Olivia's death, Allen had a life estate, the widow had a contingent remainder for life, the first child to reach 50 had a contingent remainder in fee simple, and Betty (as Olivia's sole heir) had the reversion. When Betty bought Allen's interest, she acquired the life estate. She already had the reversion. If the doctrine of destructibility of contingent remainders applies, the life estate merged with the reversion to destroy the two contingent remainders to give Betty a fee simple. Otherwise, she had only a life estate pur autre vie (which expired when Allen died) and the two future interests in fee (neither of which would become possessory until after Wilma died). Thus the viability of Wilma's suit depends on whether the doctrine of destructibility of contingent remainders is in force. Choice (A) is wrong. The Uniform Statutory Rule Against Perpetuities is irrelevant because there are no perpetuities violations in the devise. The widow's interest would vest on Allen's death. The child's interest would vest during the child's lifetime, and the child must be a life in being because this is a devise. Choice (B) is wrong. The adverse possession doctrine is irrelevant because Betty was in possession under her life estate pur autre vie. Her possession would not have been hostile to Wilma's remainder if it still existed. Choice (D) is wrong. The Doctrine of Worthier Title is not implicated by this devise because the devise did not create an express reversion in Olivia's heirs.

29. (A)

The argument in (A) is accepted by the great weight of authority. The argument in (B) will help Alan only briefly, because the limitation will soon be breached. The argument in (C) is not the strongest argument for Alan, because it recognizes some right to compensation in Ophelia's heirs. The statement in (D) is wrong.

30. (A)

If Blackacre is in a state that recognizes the doctrine of destructibility of contingent remainders, the contingent remainder must vest during Sam's life estate or it would be destroyed by the doctrine of destructibility. Therefore, the interest would not violate the Rule Against Perpetuities. But if Blackacre is in a state that does not recognize the doctrine of destructibility of contingent remainders, it is possible that Doris could have another child after the grant, all potential lives in being could end, and the after-born child could graduate from medical school more than 21 years later. Thus the contingent remainder is void ab initio under the Rule Against Perpetuities and Ann's claim would fail.

31. (A)

In a jurisdiction in which the common-law doctrine of destructibility of contingent remainders applies, the grant in (A) complies with the Rule Against Perpetuities because the child's interest will vest during Beatrice's lifetime or be destroyed at Beatrice's death. In a jurisdiction that has abolished of the doctrine of destructibility of contingent remainders, however, Beatrice's child's contingent remainder would not be destroyed at Beatrice's death, but would be converted to an executory interest. Thus there is a possibility that a child of Beatrice born after the time of the grant might pass a bar examination more than 21 years after Beatrice and all other lives in being have died. As a result, the interest violates the Rule Against Perpetuities and is destroyed ab initio in a jurisdiction in which contingent remainders are not destructible. The grant in (B) will be a term of years determinable in Charlotte followed by an executory interest in her heirs in both jurisdictions. The abolition of the Rule in Shelley's Case does not affect the grant because the rule does not apply to a term of years determinable. The grant in (C) violates the Rule Against Perpetuities in both jurisdictions because the described statutory rules do not modify the common law Rule Against Perpetuities. The grant in (D) is governed by the Doctrine of Worthier Title, which also has not been modified by the described statutory reforms.

32. (C)

On Terry's death, Arthur had a life estate, the widow had a contingent remainder for life, the first child to graduate from law school had a contingent remainder in fee simple, and Daphne (as Terry's sole heir) had the reversion. When Daphne sold her interest to Arthur, he acquired the reversion. If the doctrine of destructibility of contingent remainders applies, Arthur's life estate merged with the reversion to destroy the two contingent remainders and gave Arthur a fee simple. Otherwise, Arthur had only a life estate and the future interest in fee. Thus Wilma's suit depends entirely on the nonapplication of the doctrine of destructibility of contingent remainders. Statutory modifications of the Rule Against Perpetuities are irrelevant because there are no perpetuities violations in the devise. Similarly, the Rule in Shelley's Case and the Doctrine of Worthier Title are not implicated by this devise.

33. (B)

If Doris, Frank, and George all die before Harry, the land will revert to Teresa's heirs in fee simple on executory limitation, subject to an executory interest in the descendants still living when Harry dies. It would be difficult to sell the land outside of the family until all living members of the family die. In (A), the restraint on alienation is void. Doris will have a fee simple, which she could convey outside of the family immediately. Furthermore, the land could go to Harry as an heir of Frank or George. In (C), the remainder to Teresa's heirs accomplishes nothing. The remainder will go to Doris. If it passes to Frank and George, the land could go to Harry as an heir of Frank or George. (D) The land could go to Harry as an heir of Frank or George.

34. (D)

By eliminating the doctrine of destructibility of contingent remainders, this bill gives greater weight to the intent of grantors.

35. (B)

The gravel pit would continue producing for longer than the perpetuity period. One of the testator's after-born descendants could then claim the executory interest. There are no perpetuity violations in the other grants. In choice (A), the testator's children will take, if at all, during their own lives, and all the children of a person who has died are lives in being under RAP (even if the testator has a posthumous child). In choice (C) the eldest son will get a vested interest as soon as he is born—and that must happen during Ally's lifetime. In choice (D) Celia is a life in being for the widower's interest, Denny is his own life in being, and Ernie is a life in being for his own interest and for his heirs.

36. (B)

This question addresses the basic compromise behind every intestate succession statute: balancing the interest in having the property pass to the people that the decedent would most likely have favored with the interest in having a scheme that is administratively convenient. The best argument for this proposed legislation is administrative convenience, which is expressed in choice (B). Choice (A) is incorrect because it supports the view that decedents might prefer their property to go to the State rather than their second cousins. Choice (C) misses the point of an intestate succession statute. Choice (D) is also incorrect. Instead of allowing property to pass to "laughing heirs," the proposed legislation favors the state, not close relatives.

37. (C)

Choice (C) supports the idea that property should pass to the people who the decedent would most likely have favored. Choice (A) is incorrect. By executing a will, a person may assure that his property is distributed as he sees fit. Choice (B) is also incorrect, because the legislation will not affect the state's ability to administer it. Choice (D) is wrong. An effective intestate statute cannot be sufficiently flexible to deal with every possible complexity of a family relationship.

38. (A)

This jurisdiction has enacted an antilapse statute. Therefore, Sonny will take his mother's interest.

39. (B)

Ted intended to convey the property to Lou, who paid the agreed purchase price, and, in return, received delivery of the deed. The conveyance adeemed the gift to Doris. (B) is a better answer than (A). A prior conveyance effectively revokes a devisee's rights under a will. Also, choice (A) is not the best answer because Lou would prevail even if he acquired title to Blackacre as a gift.

40. (B)

As a devisee under the terms of Davidson's will, Alicia did not have any legal rights to his colonial-style house and its fixtures until Davidson died and his will was admitted to probate. Davidson is the legal title owner of both the colonial-style house and the condominium. As the owner, he has the power to remove whatever items he chooses and replace them in either of the two dwellings. Choice (C) is wrong because, as the fee simple owner of the property, Davidson is not liable for waste. Waste consists of an act by a life tenant or a tenant for years that results in damage to the corpus of the property. Choice (A) is also not the best answer because the fireplace did not become personalty when it was removed from the colonial-style house. Rather, Davidson intended that the fireplace remain a fixture after it was installed in the condominium.

Give the state of the title under each of the following grants, When applicable, include an analysis of each gift under both the common law RAP and USRAP. In each case, the testator began with a fee simple absolute. Identified individuals are born and ascertainable.

1. devise "to the first of my children who passes the bar examination"; testator left two children, ages five and eight

2. devise "to the first of my descendants who is elected state governor"; testator left one child, age ten

3. devise "to the first of Bart's children who becomes a violinist"; Bart who is 80, has three adult children, ages 51, 55, and 57

4. devise "to the first of Claire's sons who reaches 30"; Claire, who is 16, has no sons

5. devise "to Alice and the heirs of her body by Arthur, remainder to Boris in fee simple absolute"

6. devise "to Edward and his heirs for so long as the land is not used for commercial purposes"

7. devise "to the first of Erin's descendants to graduate from medical school"; Erin predeceased testator, leaving one child, age six

8. devise "to the first of my sons who plays major league baseball"; testator was survived by twin sons, age four

9. devise "to the first of my descendants who celebrates his or her 25th wedding anniversary"; testator was survived by two children, ages 13 and 15.

10. devise "to the first of my grandchildren who survives until his or her 21st birthday"; testator was survived by one child, age 30, who was then childless

11. devise "to the first of my grandchildren who survives until his or her 25th birthday"; testator was survived by three children, ages one, three, and six

12. devise "to the first of Gordon's sons who survives until his 30th birthday"; Gordon, who is over 80, has three adult sons, ages 22, 25, and 29

13. devise "to the first of Harry's daughters who survives until her 30th birthday"; Harry's predeceased testator, leaving one daughter, age four

14. devise "to Frederick for life, remainder to Frederick's widow for life, remainder to Geraldine for life, remainder to the heirs of Hattie; but if Hattie is still living on the death of the survivor of Frederick, Frederick's widow, and Geraldine, then to Jason and his heirs"

15. devise "to Mark and his heirs as long as he remains unmarried, remainder to Ned and his heirs"

16. devise "to Amy for life, then to Cory and his heirs for so long as he does not smoke, but if Cory starts smoking, then to Cory's heirs"

17. devise "to the first of Jason's descendants who survives until his or her 30th birthday"; Jason predeceased testator, leaving two children, ages 11 and 13

18. devise "to William and the heirs male of his body"

19. devise "to George; but if George ever sells alcoholic beverages on the land, then to Irene and her heirs"

20. devise "to the first of Lee's grandchildren who flies an airplane solo; Lee, who is 75, has two daughters, ages 50 and 52, and two grandchildren, ages 21 and 24, neither of whom has flown an airplane solo

21. devise "to the first of Mark's grandchildren who survives until his or her 21st birthday"; Mark predeceased testator, leaving two children, ages 12 and 15

22. devise "to the first of Mark's grandchildren who survives until his or her 25th birthday"; Mark predeceased testator, leaving two children, ages 12 and 15

23. devise "to Alfred for life, then to Betty for life, then to Alfred's heirs"

24. devise "to Alex for life, remainder to Alex's heirs if Alex survives Betty"

25. devise "to Stan's widow for her life, remainder in fee simple to the first of Teri's children who survives to age 30 and his or her heirs"; Stan predeceased testator, leaving an 87-year-old widow; Teri predeceased testator, leaving two children, the eldest of whom was ten at testator's death

26. devise of Whiteacre "to my eldest child then living when the limestone quarry on Whiteacre is exhausted"; at the time of the devise, testator knew that the limestone quarry would be exhausted within a few years, and the quarry was actually exhausted six years after testator's death

27. devise "to my youngest descendant living 21 years after the death of the survivor of all the descendants of Steve who are living at the time of my death"; testator was survived by three adult children and seven grandchildren; twelve of Steve's descendants were living at the time of testator's death

28. devise "to Arthur and his heirs while the premises are used for park purposes, but if the premises are not used for park purposes, the land will revert to the testator's estate"

29. devise "to Ann for life, then to John and his heirs; but if Ann farms the land, my heirs may reenter and claim the land"

1. devise "to the first of my children who passes the bar examination"; testator left two children, ages five and eight

   The devise gives testator's first child to pass the bar examination a springing executory interest in fee simple; testator's estate retains a fee simple on executory limitation. The devise does not violate the common law or statutory Rule Against Perpetuities, because the child's interest will vest, if at all, in the child's lifetime. Because the testator can have no more children after his death, the testator's children may serve as their own measuring lives.

2. devise "to the first of my descendants who is elected state governor"; testator left one child, age ten

   The devise purports to give testator's first descendant to be elected state governor a springing executory interest in fee simple; testator's estate retains a fee simple on executory limitation. Testator's child may serve as a life in being. However, this devise violates the common law Rule Against Perpetuities, however, because it may take more than 21 years after the death of that child for one of testator's descendants to be elected state governor. At common law, therefore, the entire gift is invalid and testator's estate has a fee simple.

   Under USRAP the court would uphold the interest unless none of testator's descendants is elected state governor within 90 years of testator's death.

3. devise "to the first of Bart's children who becomes a violinist"; Bart who is 80, has three adult children, ages 51, 55, and 57, none of whom has become a violinist

   The devise purports to give a springing executory interest in fee simple to the first of Bart's children who becomes a violinist. Testator's estate retains a fee simple on executory limitation. This devise violates the common law Rule Against Perpetuities. Because Bart is conclusively presumed to be capable of having more children, and because no child of Bart is yet a violinist, the rule of convenience cannot close the class of Bart's children. Therefore, Bart is the sole measuring life. It is possible that it might take more than 21 years after Bart's death for one of Bart's children to become a violinist. At common law, therefore, the entire gift is invalid and testator's estate has a fee simple.

   Under USRAP the court would uphold the interest so long as a child of Bart becomes a violinist within 90 years of testator's death.

4. devise "to the first of Claire's sons who reaches the age of 30"; Claire who is 16, has no sons

   The devise purports to give a springing executory interest in fee simple to the first of Claire's sons who reaches the age of 30. Testastor's estate retains a fee simple on executory limitation. This devise violates the common law Rule Against Perpetuities, however, because a son of Claire might reach the age of 30 more than 21 years after Claire's death. At common law, therefore, the entire gift is invalid and testator's estate has a fee simple.

Under USRAP statute, the court will uphold the interest so long as a son of Claire reaches the age of 30 within 90 years of her death.

5. devise "to Alice and the heirs of her body by Arthur, remainder to Boris in fee simple absolute"

The devise gives Alice a fee tail. Boris has a vested remainder in fee simple absolute. The devise does not violate the common law or the statutory Rule Against Perpetuities because Alice has a present possessory estate and Boris's remainder is fully vested.

6. devise "to Edward and his heirs for so long as the land is not used for commercial purposes"

Edward has a fee simple determinable, because the devise uses the phrase "for so long as," and because the limitation is built into the granting clause. The testator's estate has a possibility of reverter. Neither interest is subject to the Rule Against Perpetuities.

7. devise "to the first of Erin's descendants to graduate from medical school"; Erin predeceased the testator, leaving one child, age six

The devise purports to give the first of Erin's descendants to graduate from medical school a springing executory interest in fee simple; testator's estate retains a fee simple on executory limitation. This devise violates the common law Rule Against Perpetuities. Erin's children may serve as measuring lives, because their class closed when Erin predeceased the testator. However, it is possible that it will take more than 21 years after the deaths of Erin's children for one of Erin's descendants to graduate from medical school. At common law, therefore, the entire gift is invalid and testator's estate has a fee simple.

Under USRAP, the court would uphold the interest so long as one of Erin's descendants graduates from medical school within 90 years of the testator's death.

8. devise "to the first of my sons who plays major league baseball"; testator was survived by twin sons, age four

The devise gives a springing executory interest in fee simple to testator's first son who plays major league baseball. The testator's estate retains a fee simple on executory limitation. The devise does not violate the common law or the statutory Rule Against Perpetuities, because the interest will vest, if at all, in the lifetime of one of testator's sons. Because this devise takes effect at testator's death and testator cannot have any more sons, the testator's sons may serve as their own measuring lives.

9. devise "to the first of my descendants who celebrates his or her 25th wedding anniversary"; testator was survived by two children, ages 13 and 15

    The devise purports to give a springing executory interest in fee simple to testator's first descendant who celebrates his or her 25th wedding anniversary; testator's estate retains a fee simple on executory limitation. This devise violates the common law Rule Against Perpetuities. Because the testator is dead, the class of her children may serve as measuring lives. However, it may take more than 21 years after the death of the lives in being before the first of testator's descendants celebrates his or her 25th wedding anniversary. At common law, therefore, the entire gift is invalid and testator's estate has a fee simple.

    Under statute, the court will uphold the interest if one of testator's descendants celebrates his or her 25th wedding anniversary within 90 years of testator's death.

10. devise "to the first of my grandchildren who survives until his or her 21st birthday"; testator was survived by one child, age 30, who was then childless

    The devise gives a springing executory interest in fee simple to testator's first grandchild who survives to 21; testator's estate retains a fee simple on executory limitation. Because testator is dead, the class of testator's children may close. Therefore, testator's 30-year-old child may serve as a measuring life. Any child of testator's child will reach 21 no later than 21 years after the death of his or her parent. Therefore, the devise does not violate the common law or the statutory Rule Against Perpetuities.

11. devise "to the first of my grandchildren who survives until his or her 25th birthday"; testator was survived by three children ages one, three, and six

    The devise gives a springing executory interest in fee simple to testator's first grandchild who survives to 25. Testator's estate retains a fee simple on executory limitation. This devise violates the common law Rule Against Perpetuities. Testator's children may serve as measuring lives. However, because their class is still open, testator's grandchildren may not serve as measuring lives. It is possible that a grandchild might take more than 21 years after the death of the children to reach the age of 25. At common law, therefore, the entire gift is invalid and testator's estate has a fee simple.

    Under USRAP, the interest would be void only if a grandchild actually turned 25 more than 90 years after the death of testator's children.

12. devise "to the first of Gordon's sons who survives until his 30th birthday"; Gordon who is over 80, has three adult sons, ages 22, 25, and 29.

    The devise gives a springing executory interest in fee simple to the first of Gordon's sons who survives to 30; testator's estate retains a fee simple on executory limitation. This devise violates the common law Rule Against Perpetuities. Gordon may serve as a measuring life. However, because their class is still open, Gordon's children may not serve as measuring lives. It is possible that a child might take more than 21 years after the death of Gordon to reach the age of 30. At common law, therefore, the entire gift is invalid and testator's estate has a fee simple.

Under USRAP, the interest would be void only if a child actually turned 30 more than 90 years after Gordon's death.

13. devise "to the first of Harry's daughters who survives until her 30th birthday"; Harry's predeceased testator, leaving one daughter, age four

The devise gives a springing executory interest in fee simple to the first of Harry's daughters who survives to 30. Testator's estate retains a fee simple on executory limitation. Under USRAP, the interest would be void only if a child actually turned 30 more than 90 years after Gordon's death. The devise does not violate the common law or statutory Rule Against Perpetuities, because the daughter's interest will vest, if at all, in her own lifetime.

14. devise "to Frederick for life, remainder to Frederick's widow for life, remainder to Geraldine for life, remainder to the heirs of Hattie; but if Hattie is still living on the death of the survivor of Frederick, Frederick's widow, and Geraldine, then to Jason and his heirs"

Frederick has a life estate. Frederick's widow has a contingent remainder for life. The widow's remainder is contingent, because Frederick's widow cannot be ascertained until his death. Geraldine has a vested remainder for life. Hattie's heirs have a contingent remainder. The heirs' remainder is contingent, because Hattie's heirs cannot be ascertained until her death. Jason has an alternative contingent remainder in fee. Jason's remainder is contingent, because he will take only if Hattie is still living at the death of the survivor of Frederick, Frederick's widow, and Geraldine. The testator's estate has reversions following Geraldine's contingent life estate and the contingent remainder in Hattie's heir's. The contingent gifts do not violate the common law or statutory RAP. Frederick and Hattie are lives in being. The contingent remainder in Frederick's widow will vest, if at all, at the death of Frederick. The alternative contingent remainders in Hattie's heirs and Jason will vest, if at all, at the death of Hattie.

15. devise "to Mark and his heirs as long as he remains unmarried, remainder to Ned and his heirs"

A blanket restraint on first marriage is generally unenforceable. Restatement 2d of Property 2d, Donative Transfers § 6.1(1)—Thus, Mark has a fee simple absolute. Ned has nothing.

16. devise "to Amy for life, then to Cory and his heirs, for so long as he does not smoke"

Amy has a life estate. Cory has a vested remainder in fee simple, determinable. The testator's estate has a possibility of reverter following the determinable remainder in Cory. Cory's remainder does not violate the common law RAP or USRAP, because it is vested. The possibility of reverter in the testator's estate also does not violate the common law RAP or USRAP, because reversionary interests are not subject to RAP.

17. devise "to the first of Jason's descendants who survives until his or her 30th birthday"; Jason predeceased testator, leaving children two children, ages 11 and 13

The devise gives a springing executory interest in fee simple to the first of Jason's descendants who survives to 30. Testator's estate retains a fee simple on executory limitation. This devise violates the common law Rule Against Perpetuities. Jason may serve as a measuring life. However, because their class is still open, Jason's descendants may not serve as measuring lives. It is possible that a descendant might take more than 21 years after the death of Jason to reach the age of 30.

Under USRAP, the interest would be void only if a descendant actually turned 30 more than 90 years after Jason's death.

18. devise "to William and the heirs male of his body"

Under the common law, William has a fee tail male and the testator's estate has a reversion. Many jurisdictions have abolished the fee tail. In those jurisdictions, William has a fee simple absolute. The devise does not violate the common law or statutory Rule Against Perpetuities.

19. devise "to George; but if George ever sells alcoholic beverages on the land, then to Irene and her heirs"

George has a fee simple subject to an executory limitation in Irene. The shifting executory in Irene does not violate the common law or statutory Rule Against Perpetuities. The seisin will shift to Irene, if at all, during George's lifetime, if he sells alcoholic beverages on the premises.

20. devise "to the first of Lee's grandchildren who flies an airplane solo"; Lee, who is 75, has two daughters, ages 50 and 52, and two grandchildren, ages 21 and 24, neither of whom has flown an airplane solo

The devise gives a springing executory interest in fee simple to the first of Lee's grandchildren who flies an airplane solo. Testator's estate retains a fee simple on executory limitation. This devise violates the common law Rule Against Perpetuities. Lee may serve as a measuring life. However, because their classes are still open, neither Lee's children nor Lee's grandchildren may serve as measuring lives. It is possible that a grandchild might take more than 21 years after the death of Lee to fly an airplane solo. Under USRAP, the interest would be void if the first grandchild to fly solo does so more than 90 years after Lee's death.

21. devise "to the first of Mark's grandchildren who survives until his or her 21st birthday"; Mark predeceased testator, leaving two children, ages 12 and 15

    The devise gives a springing executory interest in fee simple to the first of Mark's grandchildren who survives to 21. Testator's estate retains a fee simple on executory limitation. The devise does not violate the the common law or statutory Rule Against Perpetuities. Because Mark predeceased the testator, the class of Mark's children is closed. Therefore, Mark's children may serve as measuring lives. The interest of the first grandchild to reach 21 will vest, if at all, within 21 years of the death of Mark's children.

22. devise "to the first of Mark's grandchildren who survives until his or her 25th birthday"; Mark predeceased testator, leaving twelve healthy children

    The devise gives a springing executory interest in fee simple to the first of Mark's grandchildren who survives to 25. Testator's estate retains a fee simple on executory limitation. This devise violates the common law Rule Against Perpetuities. Because Mark predeceased the testator, the class of Mark's children is closed. Therefore, Mark's children may serve as measuring lives. However, the interest of the first grandchild to reach 21 could vest more than 21 years of the death of Mark's children. Under USRAP, the interest would be void only if the first grandchild to reach 25 does so more than 90 years after Mark's death.

23. devise "to Alfred for life, then to Betty for life, then to Alfred's heirs"

    Under the Rule in Shelley's Case, Alfred has a life estate and a vested remainder in fee simple in Yellowacre. Betty has a vested remainder for life. None of these interests violates the common law or statutory RAP, because RAP does not apply to present possessory estates or fully vested remainders.

24. devise "to Alex for life, remainder to Alex's heirs if Alex survives Betty"

    Alex has a life estate and a contingent remainder in fee simple. Under the rule in Shelley's Case, the heirs' contingent remainder becomes Alex's contingent remainder. It is still contingent because of the survival condition. If Alex survives Betty, the remainder vests and merges with the life estate to give Alex the fee simple absolute. In the meantime, however, Alex has a life estate and a contingent remainder in fee simple in Blackacre. The testator's estate retains a reversion while the remainder remains contingent. The contingent remainder does not violate the common law or statutory RAP, because the remainder will vest, if at all, at the death of Alex.

25. devise "to Stan's widow for her life, remainder in fee simple to the first of Teri's children who survives to age 30 and his or her heirs"; Stan predeceased testator, leaving an 87-year-old widow; Teri predeceased testator, leaving two children, the eldest of whom was ten at testator's death

The devise gives Stan's widow a life estate and Teri's qualifying child a contingent remainder in fee simple. Testator's estate retains a reversion. The devise does not violate the common law or statutory Rule Against Perpetuities. The class of Teri's children closed at Teri's death. Therefore, the children may serve as measuring lives. They will reach 30, if at all, during their lifetimes.

26. devise of Whiteacre "to my eldest child then living when the limestone quarry on Whiteacre is exhausted"; at the time of the devise, testator knew that the limestone quarry would be exhausted within a few years, and the quarry was actually exhausted six years after testator's death

The devise gives the eldest surviving child a springing executory interest in fee simple. Testator's estate retains a fee simple on executory limitation. The devise does not violate the common law or statutory Rule Against Perpetuities. Because the testator is dead, the class of his children is closed. Therefore, his children may serve as their own measuring lives. To take, a child must be living when the quarry is exhausted. Thus, the child will take, if at all, by his or her own death.

27. devise "to my youngest descendant living 21 years after the death of the survivor of all the descendants of Steve who are living at the time of my death"; testator was survived by three adult children and seven grandchildren; twelve of Steve's descendants were living at the time of testator's death

The devise gives a springing executory interest in fee simple to testator's youngest descendant living 21 years after the death of the survivor of the descendants of Steve living at testator's death. Testator's estate retains a fee simple on executory limitation. The devise does not violate the Rule Against Perpetuities. The class of Steve's descendants living at the testator's death is closed at the testator's death. Therefore, the twelve then living descendants of Steve may serve as measuring lives. The testator's youngest descendant living 21 years after the death of those 12 descendants of Steve will take, if at all, at the death of those twelve living descendants.

28. devise "to Arthur and his heirs while the premises are used for park purposes, but if the premises cease to be used for park purposes, the land will revert to the testator's estate"

The use of the durational language "while" creates a fee simple determinable in Arthur. Arthur's fee simple determinable is followed by a possibility of reverter in the testator's estate. The possibility of reverter does not violate the common law or statutory Rule Against Perpetuities, because reversionary interests are not subject to RAP.

29. devise "to Ann for life, then to John and his heirs; but if Ann farms the land, my heirs may reenter and claim the land"

John holds a vested remainder subject to divestment in fee simple absolute. John holds a vested remainder because there is no condition precedent to his taking.

The remainder is subject to divestment because he may lose it before it becomes possessory (if Ann farms the land). The remainder is in fee simple absolute because if it does become possessory it will no longer be defeasible. The devise does not present any violations of the common law or the statutory Rule Against Perpetuities. Neither John's vested remainder nor the testator's estates right of reentry is subject to RAP.

Question 1

Ten years ago, Daniel, a widower, executed a typewritten will containing the following dispositive provisions:

1. I give $5,000 to my daughter, Alice.

2. I give $10,000 to my brother, John.

3. I give the residue of my estate to my sons.

Daniel signed the will at its end in the presence of two witnesses, his attorney Karen and his brother John. The witnesses signed in the presence of Daniel and in the presence of each other. At the time Daniel executed his will, he had two sons, Bill and Conor.

Two years ago, Conor died intestate, survived by his daughter Ellen.

One year ago, Daniel tore up his will, announcing that he was revoking it because he intended to execute a new will. Daniel immediately drew up a new typewritten will that was identical to the previous will, except that the gift to Alice was increased to $7,500. Daniel signed that will in the presence of his attorney, Karen, who signed the will in Daniel's presence.

Daniel recently died, leaving a net probate estate of $100,000. Daniel is survived by the following persons: Alice and Bill, Ellen, and John.

1. **May either of Daniel's wills be admitted to probate?**

2. **What rights do Alice, Bill, Ellen, and John have in Daniel's estate?**

Question 2

Ted wrote, dated, and signed his will entirely in his own handwriting. The will provided: "I want my house to go to my daughter, Sally. All my other property of any kind is to go to my wife Wilma." Sally witnessed Ted's signing and dating the will. Sally added her signature as the sole witness. At the time he executed this will, Ted owned and lived in a house on Maple Street.

Two years after Ted executed his will, his wife Wilma gave birth to their second child, Chuck. One year after the birth of Chuck, Ted sold the house on Maple Street. He immediately bought and moved his family into a larger house on Elm Street. Chuck died 25 years later, survived by his infant son, George. Two years after Chuck's death, Wilma died intestate. Shortly thereafter, Ted gave Sally $300,000 for the purchase of a home. At the time of the gift to Sally, Ted stated in writing that it was an "advancement" toward anything that Sally might take from his estate at his death. Ted died recently, survived by Sally and his grandson, George. When Ted died, his house on Elm Street was worth $200,000. His other assets were worth a total of $100,000.

1. **May Ted's will be admitted to probate?**

2. **How should the assets of Ted's estate be distributed?**

Question 3

Tanya, a widow, recently died. Her validly executed will includes the following three clauses:

1. I leave Redacre to my brother Alex for life, remainder to his widow for life, remainder to their children still living at the death of his widow.

2. I leave Whiteacre to my daughter Betty for life, remainder to grandchildren who pass a bar examination.

3. I leave Blueacre to my son Charles and his heirs for so long as the land is used for the operation of a wildlife sanctuary; but if Blueacre ceases to be used for the operation of a wildlife sanctuary, it shall pass to the Wildlife Preservation League.

At her death, Tanya was survived by two children, Betty (age 59) and Charles (age 54). Betty, who is also widowed, has one child, Portia (age 27). Portia recently passed the bar examination in her home state. Charles, who never married, has no children. Tanya's only other living relatives are her brother, Alex (age 84); Alex's two children, Margaret (age 56) and Ned (age 53); and Ned's daughter, Susan (age 19). Alex has been married for over sixty years to Zelda (age 83), and Ned has been married for almost twenty-five years to Rita (age 51).

Redacre, Whiteacre, and Blueacre are located in a jurisdiction that (a) does not require words of inheritance to create a fee simple, (b) does not recognize the doctrine of destructibility of contingent remainders, and (d) follows the common law Rule Against Perpetuities.

The jurisdiction otherwise follows common law property rules.

Please determine the validity of the devises of Redacre, Whiteacre, and Blueacre.

Question 4

Carmen, a widow, had two children, Sean and Dana. Five years ago, Carmen was informed that Sean had apparently been killed in an accident while he was travelling abroad. After she received this news, Carmen decided to execute a will. While Carmen's attorney was preparing her will, Sean sent Carmen a letter, informing her that he was alive and well but that he had decided to live in Australia for a few

years. Dana intercepted this letter and decided to conceal it from Carmen, because she wanted Carmen to omit Sean from her will. Several months later, Carmen executed a valid will that provided: "Because my son Sean has died, I leave him nothing. I leave my sister Jamie my 100 shares of XYZ Corp. stock. I leave the rest and residue of my estate to my daughter Dana." At the time she executed her will, Carmen held Blackacre as a joint tenant with her brother Tim. Carmen also held 100 shares of XYZ Corp. stock. The next year, XYZ Corp. paid Carmen a stock dividend of ten shares. Three years later, XYZ Corp. paid Carmen a $50 cash dividend.

Recently, Carmen and Tim were killed in a plane crash. All persons aboard the plane were killed instantly. Carmen's estate, exclusive of Blackacre, consisted of her original holding of 100 shares of XYZ Corp. stock, plus the ten shares distributed to her as a stock dividend, and $100,000 in cash. At the time of their death, Carmen and Tim still held Blackacre as joint tenants. Dana, Jamie, and Sean were all living at Carmen's death.

How will Carmen's estate be distributed?

Question 5

A client has asked you to draft her will. Prepare a checklist of information that you will need to gather before you draft the will. Also prepare a list of clauses that should be included in the will. In answering this question, do not address tax aspects connected with the disposition of your client's estate.

ANSWER TO QUESTION 1

1. May either of Daniel's Wills Be Admitted to Probate?

In most jurisdictions, the following formalities must be observed in the execution of a typewritten or printed will:

(1) the will must be signed at the end by the testator (or by another person at the direction of and in the presence of the testator) in the presence of at least two attesting witnesses; and

(2) in some jurisdictions, the witnesses must sign in the presence of the testator and in the presence of each other.

Formalities of Execution

Second Typewritten Will: Daniel did sign his second typewritten will in the presence of his attorney, Karen, who signed the will in his presence. However, the second will did not have a second witness. Therefore, in most jurisdictions, the second will is inadmissible.

First Typewritten Will: Daniel did sign his first typewritten will at its end in the presence of two witnesses, his sister, Karen, and his brother, John. Karen and John signed in the presence of Daniel and each other. Therefore, the execution formalities initially appear to have been met in respect to the first will.

However, in some jurisdictions, a will is not admissible into probate unless it has been subscribed by a minimum of two witnesses who were not interested in the will. A witness is interested in a will if he takes something under the will. John received a legacy of $10,000 under Daniel's first will. Therefore, John is an interested witness in that will. In a state that requires two disinterested witnesses, Daniel's first will would not be admissible into probate. However, in many states, an interested person may be a competent witness but must forfeit his interest unless he is a supernumerary witness. In such a state, John would be competent to serve as a witness (but he would forfeit his gift), and Daniel's first will would satisfy the formalities for execution.

Revocation

Revocation by Physical Act: Daniel tore up his first will immediately before he attempted to execute his second will. A will may be revoked by physical act. Physical act includes, inter alia, tearing up a will. Therefore, Daniel performed the requisite act to revoke his first will.

To cause an effective revocation, the physical act must be accompanied by intent to revoke. When he tore up his first will, Daniel announced that he was revoking that will. With that announcement, Daniel manifested the request intent to revoke. Therefore, Daniel's first will would appear to be revoked and would not be admissible into probate.

Dependent Relative Revocation: However, the doctrine of dependent relative revocation may be applied in some cases to save an otherwise revoked will. Use of the doctrine may be warranted if the testator revoked a will, based on the mistaken belief that a subsequently executed will was valid. When he tore up his first will, Daniel announced that he was revoking that will because he intended to execute a new one. However, as discussed above, the second will was not executed properly, because it had only one witness. Therefore, Daniel appears to have revoked the first will on the mistaken belief that the second will would be valid.

Dependent relative revocation is based on the notion that a decedent would prefer to die testate than intestate. To determine that preference, the court will consider evidence of the testator's schemes of distribution. Intent to die testate may be found if the several wills contained similar schemes of distribution. Daniel's first and second wills had identical schemes of distribution, except for the modest increase in Alice's gift from $5,000 to $7,500. Therefore, the probate court should find that Daniel preferred to die testate under the first will rather than to die intestate. As a result, Daniel's first will should be admitted into probate.

Conclusion on Admissibility of Wills: Daniel's second will may not be admitted into probate, because it was subscribed by only one witness. However, Daniel's first will should be admitted into probate. The will was properly executed in the majority of jurisdictions, which permit an interested person to serve as a witness to a will. The first will was revoked when Daniel tore it up. However, the first will may be saved under the doctrine of dependent relative revocation, because Daniel revoked the first will under the mistaken belief that the second will was executed properly. Therefore, the second will may be admitted into probate.

2. What rights do Alice, Bill, Ellen, and John have in Daniel's estate?

If the First Will Is Admitted into Probate

Alice: In his first will, Daniel bequeathed $5,000 to his daughter Alice. Daniel did try to increase this legacy in his second will. However, as discussed above, the second will was not executed properly. Therefore, Alice will take the $5,000 gift that Daniel left her in the first will.

Bill: Daniel devised the residue of his estate to his sons. As a surviving son of Daniel, Bill is entitled to enjoy at least half of the residue of Daniel's estate.

Ellen: Daniel's other son, Conor, predeceased Daniel. Under the common law, Conor's gift would lapse, and Bill would take the entire residue. However, if the jurisdiction has an antilapse statute, Conor's gift may be preserved. Under the typical antilapse statute, unless the will provides otherwise, a deceased beneficiary's gift will not lapse if (1) the beneficiary is a relative of the testator and (2) the beneficiary is survived by lineal descendants. In most jurisdictions, the antilapse statute applies to class gifts. Conor was Daniel's son and thus was related to the testator. Conor was survived by his daughter, Ellen, who was his lineal descendant. Therefore, Conor's gift will be preserved, and Ellen will take Conor's half of the residue by representation.

If the jurisdiction does not have an antilapse statute that applies to Conor, the gift to Conor lapsed. Under the common law "no residue of the residue" rule, if the residue is left to two or more persons and the gift to one of those person lapses, the deceased beneficiary's gift falls outside the will and passes by intestacy. However, many states have abolished the "no residue of the residue" rule. If the jurisdiction has abolished that rule, the share of the deceased beneficiary falls back into the residue and is shared by any remaining beneficiaries of the residue. Thus, if Conor's gift lapsed and the jurisdiction has abolished the "no residue of the residue" rule, Conor's share would remain in the residue. Bill, the surviving member of the residue beneficiary class, would therefore take the entire residue.

John: As discussed above, in some states, an interested witness is stripped of his gift if she is needed to satisfy the requirement for two disinterested witnesses to a will. However, in other jurisdictions, an interested witness may serve as a witness and take his gift. In such a jurisdiction, John would be entitled to receive the $10,000 legacy Daniel left to him in his will.

If Daniel's Estate Passes by Intestate Succession

If neither will is admitted into probate, Daniel's estate will pass by intestate succession. Under the typical intestate succession statute, if an intestate decedent is survived by lineal descendants but no spouse, the lineal descendants will take the entire estate. Daniel, a widower, was survived by the following lineal descendants: his children, Alice and Bill, and his granddaughter, Ellen, the child of his deceased son, Conor. The size of the intestate shares of Daniel's lineal descendants will be determined by one of three approaches: strict per stirpes, per capita with representation, and per capita at each generation. Strict per stirpes determines shares by locating the root generation, which is the first generation after the decedent. In this case, the root generation is Daniel's three children, who are the first generation after Daniel. Thus, under strict per stirpes, Daniel's estate will be divided into three shares. Under either per capita approach, the number of shares is determined by locating the first generation with survivors. In this case, the first generation with survivors is again the children, because Alice and Bill survived Daniel. Therefore, under either per capita approach, Daniel's estate will again be divided into three parts. Under either per stirpes or per capita distribution, each surviving member of the root or first generation receives a share outright. Thus, under all three approaches, Alice and Bill as surviving children will each receive 1/3 of Daniel's estate. The proper distribution of the remaining 1/3 must then be determined. Under both strict per stirpes and per capita with representation, the share of any deceased member of the root or first generation will be taken by representation by the deceased member's lineal descendants. Conor was survived by his daughter, Ellen. Therefore, under strict per stirpes and per capita with representation, Ellen will take Conor's 1/3 by representation. Under per capita at each generation, the share of a deceased member of the first generation drops down to the next generation with survivors, where it is divided equally among those survivors. Thus, under per capita at each generation, Conor's share will drop down to the grandchildren's generation, where Ellen is apparently the sole survivor. Therefore, under per capita at each generation, Ellen will also take Conor's

1/3. Thus, because the first generation after Daniel had surviving members, the result will be the same whether the jurisdiction uses the strict per stirpes, per capita with representation, or per capita at each generation approach: Alice, Bill, and Ellen will each take 1/3 of Daniel's estate.

Conclusion: Daniel's first will may be admitted to probate, because John may serve as a witness even if he was interested in the will. Although this will was revoked when Daniel tore it up, the will may nevertheless be admitted into probate under the doctrine of dependent relative revocation. Under this will, Alice will receive $5,000. Bill will take at least half of the residue. If the jurisdiction has an antilapse statute, Ellen will take the other half of the residue as the representative of her deceased father, Conor. If the jurisdiction does not have an antilapse statute that protects Conor's interest, and if the jurisdiction has abolished the "no residue of the residue" rule, Bill will take the entire residue. John will take his $10,000 legacy, if the jurisdiction permits an interested person to serve as a witness and to take under the will. If the first will is not admitted into probate, Alice, Bill, and Ellen will each take 1/3 of Daniel's estate by intestate succession.

ANSWER TO QUESTION 2

1. May Ted's will be admitted to probate?

Satisfaction of Will Formalities

In most jurisdictions, the following formalities must be observed in the execution of a typewritten or printed written will:

(1) the will must be signed at the end by the testator (or by another person at the direction of and in the presence of the testator) in the presence of at least two attesting witnesses; and

(2) in some jurisdictions, the witnesses must sign in the presence of the testator and in the presence of each other. Ted did sign his will. However, the will was witnessed by only one person, Sally. Therefore, Ted's will does not satisfy the typical formalities for admission into probate.

Holographic Will: Approximately half of the jurisdictions recognize holographic wills. Traditionally, a holographic will has been defined as a will that is entirely in the handwriting of the testator. The Uniform Probate Code expands the definition to include a will with the signature and material portions of the document in the testator's handwriting. Ted's will was entirely in his handwriting. Therefore, the will should qualify as a holographic will in any jurisdiction that recognizes holographic wills.

As discussed above, Ted's will was subscribed by only one witness, Sally. Further, Sally received Ted's house under the will, which rendered her an interested witness. However, under the U.P.C. and in jurisdictions in which it is recognized, a holographic will is admissible even if it does not bear the signatures of subscribing witnesses. Therefore, in a jurisdiction that recognizes holographic wills, the admissibility of Ted's will is not affected by the lack of a second witness or Sally's interest in the will.

Conclusion on Admissibility of Ted's Will: Because it was subscribed by only one witness, Ted's will did not satisfy typical statutory will formalities. However, because it was made entirely in Ted's handwriting, the will should be admissible as a holographic will, if the jurisdiction recognizes that type of will.

2. How should the assets of Ted's estate be distributed?

If Ted's Will Is Admitted into Probate

Sally:

<u>Interested Witness</u>: In his will, Ted devised his house to Sally, who was also a witness to Ted's will. As discussed above, a holographic will does not require witnesses. Therefore, Sally's interest has no effect on the admissibility of the will. As a result, Sally is qualified to take a gift under Ted's will.

<u>Ademption</u>: The question becomes whether Sally's gift was adeemed by extinction. Property that is to be disposed of in a will is adeemed by extinction if it is no longer in the testator's estate at the time of his death. When he executed his will, Ted owned and lived in a house on Maple Street. However, when he died, Ted no longer owned or lived in the Maple Street house. Thus, the gift of the house to Sally may appear to have been adeemed.

However, a will may dispose of property by reference to acts and events that have significance apart from their effect on the dispositions made by the will. Ted's move from the house on Maple Street to the larger house on Elm Street was an act that had significance independent of the disposition that he had made in his will. When a testator makes a change in property that is independent of a disposition that he has made in his will, the devisee will receive the property in the testator's estate that matches the description, even if it is not the property that was in the testator's estate at the time the will was executed. Thus, the devise to Sally should be comprised of the house that was in Ted's estate when he died, which is the Elm Street house.

<u>Satisfaction</u>: Under the Uniform Probate Code, if a testator makes a gift to a will beneficiary during the testator's lifetime, the gift may be considered to be in whole or partial satisfaction of the testate gift if the inter vivos gift falls into any one of the following three categories:

(1) The testator's will provides that the inter vivos gift satisfies the devise;

(2) the inter vivos gift is accompanied by a writing that confirms that the inter vivos gift is intended to be in satisfaction of the testamentary devise; or

(3) the recipient of the inter vivos gift acknowledges in writing that the gift was made in satisfaction of the testamentary devise. Ted did make an inter vivos gift

of $300,000 to Sally. At the time he made the gift, he called it an "advancement" toward anything that Sally might take from his estate at his death. Although he did not use the term "satisfaction," Ted clearly intended the gift to be in satisfaction of Sally's testamentary devise. Therefore, in at least some jurisdictions, the gift of $300,000 may be counted against the value of the house, which was $200,000. In those jurisdictions, because the value of the satisfaction exceeds the value of the devise, Sally will take nothing under Ted's will.

However, in at least some jurisdictions, the doctrine of satisfaction is not applied when the testamentary gift is a specific devise of real property. In those jurisdictions, a specific devise of real property may be satisfied only by an inter vivos gift of that same real property. In such a jurisdiction, the gift to Sally of $300,000 in cash would not be deemed to be in satisfaction of the devise of the house to Sally. As a result, in such jurisdictions, Sally will be entitled to both the $300,000 inter vivos gift and the devised house on Elm Street.

Wilma: Ted left the residue of his estate to Wilma. However, Wilma predeceased Ted. Therefore, Wilma's gift lapsed, unless it was protected by an antilapse statute. Under the typical antilapse statute, unless the will provides otherwise, a deceased beneficiary's gift will not lapse if (1) the beneficiary is a relative of the testator and (2) the beneficiary is survived by lineal descendants. In the context of an antilapse statute, the term "relative" generally does not include a spouse. Therefore, Wilma is not likely to be protected, regardless of the type of antilapse statute in effect in this jurisdiction. Because Wilma is not protected, her gift of the residue lapses, and the remainder of Ted's estate will pass by intestacy. (See the discussion below.)

Chuck: A pretermitted child is a child born to a testator after the testator executes a will. Typically, a pretermitted child may take her intestate share against the will. Because he was born after Ted executed his will, Chuck appears to be a pretermitted child. However, Chuck died before Ted. The protection of the pretermitted child doctrine generally does not extend to issue of a pretermitted child who predeceased the testator. Therefore, Chuck's son George will not be able to take Chuck's pretermitted child's share.

Intestacy

Ted's entire estate will pass by intestate succession if (1) the jurisdiction does not recognize holographic wills, or (2) the jurisdiction recognizes holographic wills but the gift of the residue to Wilma lapses and the gift of "my house" to Sally is considered satisfied by the inter vivos gift of $300,000 to her. If the holographic will is admitted to probate and the devise of the house is not satisfied by the $300,000 inter vivos gift to Sally, the residue of Ted's estate will nevertheless pass by intestate succession, because the gift of the residue to Wilma lapsed.

Under the typical intestate succession statute, if an intestate decedent is survived by lineal descendants but no spouse, the lineal descendants will take the entire estate. Ted was a widower at his death, and he was survived by two lineal descendants, his daughter, Sally, and his grandson, George, who is the son of Ted's deceased son Chuck.

The size of the intestate shares of Ted's lineal descendants will be determined by one of three approaches: strict per stirpes, per capita with representation, and per capita at each generation. Strict per stirpes determines shares by locating the root generation, which is the first generation after the decedent. In this case, the root generation is Ted's two children, who are the first generation after Ted. Thus, under strict per stirpes, Ted's estate would be divided into two shares. Under either per capita approach, the number of shares is determined by locating the first generation with survivors. In this case, the first generation with survivors is again the children, because Sally survived Ted. Therefore, under the per capita approach, Ted's estate will again be divided into two parts. Under either per stirpes or per capita distribution, each surviving member of the root or first generation receives a share outright. Thus, under all three approaches, Sally as a surviving child will each receive 1/2 of Ted's estate. The proper distribution of the remaining 1/2 must then be determined. Under both strict per stirpes and per capita with representation, the share of any deceased member of the root or first generation will be taken by representation by the deceased member's lineal descendants. Chuck was survived by his son, George. Therefore, under strict per stirpes and per capita with representation, George will take Chuck's 1/2 by representation. Under per capita at each generation, the share of a deceased member of the first generation drops down to the next generation with survivors, where it is divided equally among those survivors. Thus, Chuck's share would drop down to the grandchildren's generation, where George is apparently the sole survivor. Therefore, under per capita at each generation, George would also take Chuck's 1/2. Thus, because the first generation after Ted had a surviving member, the result will be the same whether the jurisdiction uses the strict per stirpes, per capita with representation, or per capita at each generation approach: Sally and George will each take 1/2 of Ted's estate. If the entire net estate of $300,000 passes by intestacy, Sally and George would each be assigned $150,000, reduced by debts and the cost of administration. If Sally takes the $200,000 house and only the $100,000 residue passes by intestacy, Sally and George would each be assigned $50,000, reduced by debts and administrative costs.

Advancement: However, Sally's intestate share may be affected by the $300,000 inter vivos gift she received from Ted. An advancement is an inter vivos transfer to a potential beneficiary that occurs before the intestate death of the decedent. Ted did make an inter vivos transfer to a potential beneficiary of his intestate estate when he gave Sally $300,000 for the purchase of a home. A transfer will be treated as an advancement if the decedent declared in a contemporaneous writing or the heir acknowledged in writing that the gift is an advancement. At the time he gave the money to Sally, Ted did declare in writing that the gift was "advancement" toward anything that Sally might take from his estate at his death. Therefore, the $300,000 given to Sally during Ted's lifetime should be deemed an advancement toward her intestate share.

Hotchpot: The effect of the advancement on Sally's intestate share is determined through a process called hotchpot. Under hotchpot, the value of the advancement is first added back into the intestate estate. If Ted's entire estate passes by intestacy, the total of the hotchpot is $600,000 ($300,000 probate estate plus $300,000 advancement). If only the residue of Ted's estate passes by intestacy, the total of the hotchpot is $400,000 ($100,000 probate estate plus $300,000 advancement).

Next, the hotchpot share of each taker is determined by dividing the hotchpot by the number of takers. In this case, the number of takers is two (Sally and George). If the entire estate passes by intestacy, the hotchpot share of each taker is $300,000. If only the residue passes by intestacy, the hotchpot share of each taker is $200,000.

To determine final distribution, the advancement is then subtracted from the hotchpot share of the taker who received the advancement. The $300,000 advancement exceeds or is equal to Sally's hotchpot share ($300,000 for total intestacy, and $200,000 for partial intestacy). Therefore, whether the entire estate passes by intestacy, or only the residue passes by intestacy, Sally is not entitled to an intestate distribution. As a result, if the $300,000 inter vivos gift to Sally counts as an advancement, George will take the entire intestate estate, reduced by debts and costs of administration.

Conclusion on Distribution of Ted's Estate: If Ted's holographic will is admitted to probate, Sally should take the house on Elm Street, unless the jurisdiction applies the rules of satisfaction to specific devises of real property. Because a holographic will need not be witnessed, Sally's status as an interested witness will have no effect on her gift. Wilma will take nothing under Ted's will, because she predeceased Ted and is not as a predeceasing spouse likely to be protected by an antilapse statute. Chuck, who was born after Ted executed his will, may not be protected as a pretermitted child because he predeceased Ted.

Ted's entire estate will pass by intestate succession if (1) the jurisdiction does not recognize holographic wills, or (2) the gift of the residue to Wilma lapses and the gift of the house to Sally was satisfied by the inter vivos gift to her. If the holographic will is admitted to probate and the devise of the house is not satisfied by the inter vivos gift to Sally, the residue of Ted's estate will nevertheless pass by intestate succession, because the gift of the residue to Wilma lapsed. As the only surviving lineal descendants of Ted, Sally, and George will be assigned half shares of the intestate distribution. However, Sally received an advancement that was equal to or exceeded her hotchpot share. Therefore, George will take the entire intestate estate, reduced by debts and costs of administration.

ANSWER TO QUESTION 3

1. Validity of Devise of Redacre

In clause 1 of her will, Tanya made the following devise: "I leave Redacre to my brother Alex for life, remainder to his widow for life, remainder to their children still living at the death of his widow."

Nature of Interests Created: In assessing this devise under the Rule Against Perpetuities, the first step is to determine the nature of the interests created. On the death of Tanya, the following interests were created. Alex received a present possessory life estate in Redacre. The widow of Alex received a contingent remainder for life. A remainder is contingent if (1) the taker is unascertained, or (2) there is a condition precedent to the vesting of the remainder. Because Alex is still living, the identity of his widow cannot yet be determined. Therefore, the taker of this remainder is unascertained. As a result, the widow's remainder for life is contingent. The children of Alex and his widow also have a contingent remainder. The interest of the children is subject to a condition precedent, because the children must be living at the death of the widow. Therefore, the children of Alex and his widow have a contingent remainder in fee simple absolute. Because the last interest in the devise is a contingent remainder, a reversion is also given to Tanya's estate.

Validity of Interests under the Common Law Rule against Perpetuities

<u>Interests Subject to RAP</u>: The next step is to determine which of the interests created in the devise is subject to the Rule Against Perpetuities. Present possessory interests are not subject to RAP. Therefore, the present possessory life estate held by Alex is not subject to RAP. Contingent remainders are subject to RAP. As explained above, the widow and the children have contingent remainders. Therefore, the future interests of the widow and the children are subject to RAP. Reversionary interests are not subject to RAP. Therefore, the reversion in Tanya's estate is not subject to RAP.

<u>Life or Lives In Being/Measuring Lives</u>: The validity of the contingent remainders will be measured against lives in being. Lives in being are persons who were alive and ascertained at the time the interests are created. In this case, the interests were created at Tanya's death, when the will that created the interests took effect. At the moment of Tanya's death, Alex was alive and may constitute an express life in being. At that time, Alex was married to Zelda. However, Zelda could not then qualify as Alex's widow, because he was still alive. Because the widow was not then ascertained, the widow may not serve as a life in being. At the time of Tanya's death, Alex was 84 and had two middle-aged children, Margaret and Ned. Members of a class may not serve as measuring lives unless their class is closed. Under the common law RAP, a person is conclusively presumed to be capable of having more children. Therefore, despite his advanced age, Alex is presumed to be capable of having more children. As a result, the class of his children cannot yet close, which means that neither Margaret nor Ned may serve as a measuring life. Thus, Alex is the only measuring life in respect to this devise.

<u>Vesting Within 21 Years of the Life In Being</u>: Under the common law RAP, vesting or failing is judged according to the "might have been" rule. Under this rule, an interest violates RAP if it is even remotely possible for the interest to vest, if at all, more than 21 years after a life in being. Alex's widow will take, if at all, immediately on the death of Alex, who is the measuring life. Therefore, the widow's contingent remainder for life is valid under RAP.

The contingent remainder in the children living at the death of the widow presents the classic "unborn widow" scenario. Alex has been married to Zelda for over 60 years. Nevertheless, Zelda could die or divorce Alex. Alex could then remarry a young woman who was not even born at the time devise took effect (at the death of Tanya). That young woman could live more than 21 years after Alex's death. Thus, it is possible, although not likely, that Alex's children could take Redacre more than 21 years after the death of Alex, who is the measuring life. As a result, the contingent remainder in the children violates RAP.

Voiding of Gift That Violates RAP: If a gift violates RAP, the gift is treated as void ab initio. After the interest in the children is voided, the following interests are left in effect: a present possessory life estate in Alex, a contingent remainder for life in Alex's widow, and a reversion in Tanya's estate.

2. Validity of Devise of Whiteacre

In clause 2 of her will, Tanya made the following devise: "I leave Whiteacre to my daughter Betty for life, remainder to my grandchildren who pass a bar examination."

Nature of Interests Created: In assessing this devise under the Rule Against Perpetuities, the first step is to determine the nature of the interests created. On the death of Tanya, the following interests were created. Betty receives a presently possessory life estate in Whiteacre. A remainder may be given to a class, such as grandchildren. A remainder to a class is vested subject to open if at least one member of the class is ascertained and has fulfilled any conditions precedent to the vesting of the remainder. Portia is a member of the class of Tanya's grandchildren and Portia has fulfilled the condition precedent of passing a bar examination. Although Tanya had no other grandchildren at her death, under the common law, her children Betty and Charles are conclusively presumed to be capable of having more children. Further, as discussed below, the Rule of Convenience may not be used at this time to close the class of Tanya's grandchildren who pass a bar examination. Therefore, Portia holds for Tanya's grandchildren a remainder that is vested subject to open.

Validity of Interests under the Common Law Rule against Perpetuities

Interests Subject to RAP: The next step is to determine which of the interests created in the devise is subject to the Rule Against Perpetuities. Present possessory interests are not subject to RAP. Therefore, the present possessory life estate held by Betty is not subject to RAP. A remainder that is vested subject to open is subject to RAP, unless the class may be closed early under the Rule of Convenience.

Under the Rule of Convenience, a class closes when a member of the class is entitled to distribution. A member of the class who is born or conceived at the time the class closes may participate in the gift, if and when she fulfills any conditions precedent to the vesting of the gift. Portia has fulfilled the condition precedent of passing a bar examination. However, she is not yet entitled to distribution, because Betty is currently enjoying her life estate. Therefore, the remainder in the grandchildren remains vested subject to open and is consequently subject to RAP.

Life or Lives In Being/Measuring Lives: The validity of the contingent remainders will be measured against lives in being. Lives in being are persons who were alive and ascertained at the time the interests are created. In this case, the interests were created at Tanya's death, when the will that created the interests took effect. At the moment of Tanya's death, Betty was alive and may constitute an express life in being. At the time of Tanya's death, Portia, her grandchild, was also alive. Members of a class may not serve as measuring lives unless their class is closed. As discussed above, the class of Tanya's grandchildren was not closed at her death. Therefore, Portia may not serve as a life in being. Thus, Betty is the only measuring life in respect to this devise.

<u>Vesting within 21 Years of the Life In Being</u>: Under the common law RAP, vesting or failing is judged according to the "might have been" rule. Under this rule, an interest violates RAP if it is even remotely possible for the interest to vest, if at all, more than 21 years after a life in being. At her death, Tanya had only one grandchild, Portia, who has already passed a bar examination. Although both Betty and Charles were both middle-aged at Tanya's death, they are conclusively presumed to be capable of having children throughout their lives. Therefore, it is possible that Betty or Charles will subsequently have a child who will pass a bar examination more than 21 years after Betty dies. As a result, the interest in the grandchildren violates RAP.

<u>Voiding of Gift That Violates RAP</u>: If a gift violates RAP, the gift is treated as void ab initio. After the interest in the grandchildren is voided, the following interests are left in effect: a present possessory life estate in Betty and a reversion in Tanya's estate.

3. Validity of Devise of Blueacre

In clause 3 of her draft will, Tanya made the following devise: "I leave Blueacre to my son Charles and his heirs for so long as the land is used for a wildlife sanctuary; but if Blueacre ceases to be used for a wildlife sanctuary, it shall pass to the Wildlife Preservation League."

Nature of Gifts Created: In assessing this devise under the Rule Against Perpetuities, the first step is to determine the nature of the interests created. On the death of Tanya, the following interests were created. Charles received a fee simple subject to an executory limitation, a type of defeasible estate. A present possessory defeasible estate is one that is presently enjoyed but that may be defeased on the happening of a certain event. In this case, Charles is presently enjoying his estate in Blueacre. However, Charles could lose his estate if Blueacre ceases to be used as a wildlife sanctuary. Therefore, Charles has a fee simple subject to an executory limitation. The Wildlife Preservation League has the executory interest that follows Charles' defeasible fee. A future interest is a shifting executory interest if it cuts short the preceding estate, causing the seisin to shift from one third person to another. The future interest in the Wildlife Preservation League may cut short Charles' estate if Blueacre is not used as a wildlife sanctuary. If Charles' estate is cut short, the seisin will shift from Charles to the Preservation League. Therefore, the Preservation League has a shifting executory interest.

Validity of Interests under the Common Law Rule against Perpetuities

<u>Interests Subject to RAP</u>: The next step is to determine which of the interests created in the devise is subject to the Rule Against Perpetuities. Present possessory interests are not subject to RAP. Therefore, the present possessory life estate held by Charles is not subject to RAP. Executory interests are subject to RAP. As explained above, the Wildlife Preservation League has an executory interest. Therefore, the Preservation League's future is subject to RAP.

Life or Lives In Being/Measuring Lives: The validity of the executory interests will be measured against lives in being. Lives in being are persons who were alive and ascertained at the time the interests are created. In this case, the interests were created at Tanya's death, when the will that created the interests took effect. At the moment of Tanya's death, Charles was alive and may constitute an express life in being. Measuring lives must be natural persons. The Preservation League is an organization, not a person. Therefore, Charles is the only measuring life in respect to this devise.

Vesting Within 21 Years of the Life In Being: Under the common law RAP, vesting or failing is judged according to the "might have been" rule. Under this rule, an interest violates RAP if it is even remotely possible for the interest to vest, if at all, more than 21 years after a life in being. It is possible that an heir of Charles may cease to use Blueacre as a wildlife sanctuary more than 21 years after Charles dies. Therefore, the executory interest in the Preservation League violates RAP.

The devise to the Preservation League may not be saved by the Charity to Charity exception to RAP. Under this exception, an executory interest that would otherwise violate RAP may be preserved if the seisin shifts from one charity to another. The Preservation League appears to be a charity. However, Charles is an individual, not a charity. Because the seisin would not shift from a charity to the Preservation League (a charity), the future interest of the Preservation League cannot be saved under the Charity to Charity exception.

Voiding of Gift That Violates RAP: If a gift violates RAP, the gift is treated as void ab initio. After the interest in the Preservation League is voided, the following interests are left in effect. Charles has a fee simple determinable. A fee simple determinable is created by the use of the words "for so long as" and by building the limitation into the clause that creates the interest. Tanya devised Blueacre "to Charles for so long as the land is used as a wildlife sanctuary...." The devise used the words "for so long as," and the sanctuary limitation on the use was built into the clause that created Charles' fee. Therefore, Charles received a fee simple determinable. Following that fee simple determinable, a possibility of reverter was created in Tanya's estate.

ANSWER TO QUESTION 4

How will Carmen's Estate Be Distributed?

Probate of Carmen's Will

Carmen omitted her son Sean intentionally from her will, because she thought he died during his trip abroad. Therefore, Sean may participate in Carmen's estate only if he is able to prevent Carmen's will from being admitted into probate. Sean may seek to prevent probate of the will by alleging that (1) Carmen was mistaken when she omitted him from her will or (2) Dana fraudulently induced Carmen to omit Sean from the will.

Mistake of Omission

A mistake of omission occurs when the testator omits a person from his will due to a mistaken belief of fact. For example, a testator may omit a gift for a relative because the testator mistakenly believes that the relative is dead. Carmen omitted a gift for Sean because she mistakenly believed that he was dead. Therefore, Carmen made a mistake of omission when she executed her will.

Mistake of fact that results in an omission generally does not affect the enforcement of a will. Therefore, in most jurisdictions, Carmen's will may be admitted to probate as written, despite her mistake concerning Sean's death. However, some courts may deny probate of a will if the mistake is clear from the face of the will. Carmen's will clearly demonstrates her mistaken belief about Sean's death, because the will states "[b]ecause my son Sean has died, I leave him nothing." Therefore, it is possible that some courts might decline to admit Carmen's will into probate.

Fraud in the Inducement

Fraud in the inducement occurs when a person uses fraud to induce a person to execute a contract or a will. However, fraud in the inducement that results in an omission from a will does not affect the enforcement of that will. Dana did fraudulently hide from Carmen the letter informing Carmen that Sean was still alive. However, Dana's fraud resulted in the omission from Carmen's will of a gift to Sean. Therefore, Dana's fraud will not prevent the probate of Carmen's will (However, Sean might be able to have a constructive trust imposed on Dana, because she obtained the property through fraud in the inducement. In addition, Sean might also have a cause of action against Dana for interference with a prospective economic advantage.)

Conclusion on Admissibility of Carmen's Will to Probate: In most jurisdictions, neither the mistake of omission nor Dana's fraudulent inducement will be sufficient to prevent the probate of Carmen's will.

Distribution of Estate Under Carmen's Will

Joint Tenancy in Blackacre

At the time of her death, Carmen held Blackacre as a joint tenant with her brother Tim. Carmen and Tim died together in an airplane crash. Therefore, the distribution of Blackacre will be governed by the Simultaneous Death Act. Under that act, if it is not possible to determine which of two persons died first, the property of each person will pass as if that person survived the other person. When two joint tenants die simultaneously, the property will be divided, with one half assigned to each of the two joint tenants. The half of the property assigned to each joint tenant will then be distributed as if that tenant had survived the other. Thus, Blackacre will be divided into two parts, one assigned to Carmen and the other to Tim. Carmen's one half will be distributed as if Carmen had survived Tim. Because Carmen's will did not include a devise of this property interest, Carmen's one-half share will pass through the residuary clause to Dana.

XYZ Corp. Stock and Dividends

Carmen devised "my 100 shares of XYZ Corp. stock" to her sister Jamie. At the time of her death, Carmen still held the 100 shares of XYZ stock that she owned when she executed the will. She also held an additional 10 shares of XYZ Corp. stock, which she received as a stock dividend after she executed her will. Because she used the words "my 100 shares," Carmen made a specific bequest of the stock to Jamie. Jamie will take the 100 shares, because they were still in Carmen's possession when she died. Under the Uniform Probate Code, if a testator makes a general or a specific devise of stock, in addition to the stock remaining at the time of the testator's death, the devisee will receive additional stock acquired by a stock split or a stock dividend. Therefore, Jamie will also take the additional 10 shares of stock distributed to Carmen as a stock dividend after Carmen executed her will. However, the devisee is not entitled to cash dividends paid on the stock before the death of the testator. Therefore, Jamie will not receive the $50 cash dividend paid by XYZ Corp. to Carmen after she executed her will.

$100,000 Cash

When she died, Carmen had $100,000 in cash. After creditors and the costs of administration have been paid, the remaining cash will pass through the residuary clause to Dana.

Conclusion on Distribution of Carmen's Estate under Her Will: By operation of the Simultaneous Death Act, one-half of Blackacre will pass to Dana through the residuary clause of Carmen's will. By specific bequest, Jamie will receive Carmen's 100 shares of XYZ Corp. stock, plus the additional 10 shares of XYZ Corp. stock that Carmen received as a stock dividend. After the payment of creditors and the cost of administration, Carmen's remaining cash will be distributed to Dana through the residuary clause.

Distribution of Carmen's Estate by Intestate Succession

If, for any reason, Carmen's will is not admitted to probate, her estate will pass by intestacy. When she died, Carmen was a widow and was survived by her children, Dana and Sean, and her sister, Jamie. Under the Uniform Probate Code, if a decedent is survived by lineal descendants but no spouse, the decedent's estate will be divided between or among the lineal descendants. Therefore, if Carmen's estate passes by intestate succession, her children, Dana and Sean will each take 1/2 of the estate. Because she is a collateral heir, Jamie will take nothing by intestacy.

ANSWER TO QUESTION 5

Checklist of information needed to draft a will.

The following information should be gathered by an attorney before she drafts a will for a client.

Names and contact information for beneficiaries

The client should supply the names and contact information for all persons or organizations to be named as beneficiaries in the will.

Relationship of beneficiaries to the client

The relationship of each beneficiary to the client must be documented.

Marital status of the client

The marital status of the client must be determined. If the client is married, the existence of a prenuptial or postnuptial agreement must be determined. The age and mental and physical health of the spouse should also be established, particularly if the spouse suffers from a disability that requires continuing care.

The age and mental and physical health of the client's children

The age of each child must be noted, particularly if a child is a minor. The mental and physical health of each child should be determined, especially if a child suffers from a disability that requires continuing care.

Name and contact information for the person or financial institution to be appointed personal representative or executor

The name and contact information should be gathered for the person or entity that will be appointed personal representative of the client's estate.

State of domicile

The state of domicile must be established. The attorney must also determine whether the state follows common law or community property principles.

Estate assets

The client must detail the assets of her estate. This detail should be documented in a property inventory that lists the following: the location and contents of her bank accounts, the legal description of all real estate owned by the client, all motor vehicles that are registered to the client, tangible and intangible personal property owned by the client, retirement accounts and life insurance policies owned by the client, debts owed by the client, and intellectual property or partnership interests owned by the client.

Time frame for drafting the will

The client must indicate the time frame under which the will must be prepared.

Clauses to be included in the will.

Testimonium

The will should begin with a testimonium clause that confirms that the client is of sound mind and declares the document to be her last will and testament.

Revocation clause

To assure that the will overrides any previous testamentary documents, the will should include a clause revoking all previous wills and codicils.

List of specific gifts

The will should list all specific devises and bequests. To avoid lapse issues, alternative takers should also be listed.

List of general bequests

The will should also list all general bequests or legacies. To avoid lapse issues, alternative takers should also be listed.

Residuary clause

The will should also include a residuary clause that disposes of any part of the client's estate not otherwise specifically devised in the will.

Survivorship provision

The will should include a clause stating the period of time for which a beneficiary must survive the testator (e.g., 45 days). An alternative beneficiary should be named to take if the beneficiary predeceases the testator or does not survive for the requisite period following the testator's death.

Executor or personal representative

The will should include a clause that names and identifies the person the client has chosen as the executor or personal representative of her will. In addition, the will should specify the rights and duties of the executor or personal representative and any compensation due the executor or personal representative.

Personal and/or property guardian

If the client has minor children, the will should appoint guardians to care for them and to manage their inheritances. The guardianship clause should include the names of the guardians the client has chosen as well as alternate guardians.

Trustee

If the client has minor children, the will should appoint a trustee to manage any trust the client has established for her children.

Severability clause

The will should include a severability clause to assure the admissibility of the rest of the will if one section of the will fails.

Signature section

The will must include a section for the client's signature, the date, and the city, state, and county.

Witnesses section

The will must also include a section for witnesses' signature, the date, and the city, state, and county.

Notary

To assist in the authentication of the will, a notarization section should also be included.

Self-proving affidavit

To assist further in the authentication of the will, a self-proving affidavit should be attached to the will. This affidavit should state that the testator was of sound mind, understood that the document she was signing was her will, and signed it as a voluntary act. The affidavit should also state that the will was witnessed by the witnesses. The affidavit should be signed by the testator and the witnesses and notarized.

NOTES

KAPLAN pmbr

NOTES

KAPLAN) pmbr

NOTES

KAPLAN) *pmbr*

NOTES

KAPLAN **pmbr**